# The
# SPIRIT
## of the
# RIVER

# The SPIRIT of the RIVER

## A Quest for the KINGFISHER

# DECLAN MURPHY

THE LILLIPUT PRESS
*Dublin*

First published 2021 by

THE LILLIPUT PRESS LTD

62–63 Sitric Road, Arbour Hill, Dublin 7, Ireland

www.lilliputpress.ie

ISBN 978 1 84351 80 20

A CIP record is available from the British Library.

1 3 5 7 9 10 8 6 4 2

The Lilliput Press gratefully acknowledges the financial support
of the Arts Council/An Chomhairle Ealaíon.

Typeset by Niall McCormack

Printed in Spain by Graphy Cems

# CONTENTS

# FOREWORD

Ireland; County Wicklow; Avoca; Dale House; Merrigan's Field; Mount Platt; the Meetings of the Waters – all words so familiar to me, yet places I have yet to see and visit. These words, along with the Avoca Mines, run through the heart of my family.

My grandpa Jim is a geologist who took his family to live in the Vale of Avoca. They lived in Dale House, surrounded by lawns, a huge vegetable garden, a giant apple tree and a rocky hill covered in rhododendrons and bracken. At the bottom of the drive was a small orchard and a stream that ran parallel down the hill in Ballygahan to the Avoca river. Nature was everywhere and my mum told me of hours spent out walking through the woods and fields and going to her secret place in the garden, a huge rhododendron where she would perch on a bough that was her seat.

From my earliest moments I have been drawn to nature. My first words were the the *kak kak kak* I copied from the magpie family that live near my house in north London. I was drawn to the row of lavender at our best friends' Manuela and Julian's house as soon as I could walk and the thousands, or so it seemed to me, honeybees that would visit for their daily feast. The present from Julian every year of his honeybees' precious honey is a memory that always takes me back to our London home.

Grandpa Jim truly is a tree of knowledge. He has travelled the world and has shared with me all his stories, from his great escape from a bull elephant to his snake encounters in Africa, rescuing a sloth as it crossed a mining road and outswimming a water monitor lizard and the great sight of millions of flamingos over Lake Tanganyika. He grew up in Port Isaac in Cornwall and here began his tremendous knowledge of birds. Like Declan and his quest for the kingfisher, my grandfather's quest was to see the puffins at St Kilda, a boyhood dream he fulfilled with my grandmother when they were both in their sixties. To celebrate they climbed to the highest point on the island and shouted that they were the King and Queen of the World.

Grandpa Jim has shared his great knowledge and love of nature and its animals with me and so sparked my enquiring mind, allowing me to ask as many questions as I want. He almost always has the answer and if he doesn't, he has amongst his hundreds of books one that can give me the answer. Grandpa has a giant family atlas that my mother remembers from when she was a child and inside are some well-thumbed page, one of which is Ireland. And there on the page, as I scan down, next to Arklow is Avoca, with the blue of the rivers prominent and streaking through the green to the sea.

As an environmentalist I feel great empathy and emotion with a lot of Declan's words as he talks about his childhood. I understand his constant search for knowledge and needing answers to the hows and the whys. The theme of family runs through his book not only just for himself but also the closeness and care he feels for every animal, bird and insect he comes across. His desire to learn more and feed his need to be amongst nature was satisfied to a point by the love and care of his family. Walks along the stream, holidays in woodlands and nature books stacked on every surface in his room. Even though his parents didn't understand his craving for knowledge about nature, they supported him in all he did. I feel it completely when I read the first chapters. Declan's family were always protective of him and in doing so helped him and enabled him as he grew up and made nature his life's work.

Walking through the tall grass along the river with Declan as I read his words was pure joy to me. I could see the dippers and the woodpeckers and the halcyon streak of blue. As I read every day I looked forward to the adventures of the birds. I spoke with my Grandpa Jim about the river and he told me where he thought the places might be and his memories of the river in Wicklow and the nature around it. He has many bird books and showed me pictures of all the birds that were now, because of Declan's words, so familiar to me. Even his use of onomatopoeia to illustrate the call of the birds makes the book come alive.

When I met Jane Goodall, she told me the story of how trees communicate with each other, and from that moment I have never walked through a wood in the same way. I started noticing how fallen trees still grow new shoots and how these trees are fed by the others around them. Declan mentions the unnoticed birds that aren't so colourful yet their daily life is as busy and remarkable as their beautifully coloured feathered friends. These words have stayed with me and I have made a point since finishing the book whenever I am out walking in the woods to make time to listen and notice as many of their songs as I can and paying attention to exactly what the birds are doing. My eyes are now noticing their subtle colours more intently and hearing their individual songs in the wood that is their theatre.

Thank you Declan for sharing your journey along the river, and letting me delve into the lives of the dipper, the woodpecker, the wagtails, the kingfisher and the goosander, the fox, the otter and the mink. The daily lives of this animal community is surely a nature series in itself. This book is a joy from word to word and I heartily recommend it to be on every school's reading list. Any budding naturalist will be thrilled to have a copy.

*Lilly Platt, February 2021*
*Global Youth Environmentalist and Activist*

# INTRODUCTION

MY PREVIOUS BOOK, *A Life in the Trees*, came about as a result of my interest in the great spotted woodpecker. However, that species' story, and my interest in it, did not finish with that book's conclusion. I continued to follow the lives of those woodpeckers and was delighted to discover that they still had many new secrets to share with me in the years that followed.

Throughout my writing of that book, I watched and tracked other animals with the same keenness, but there were simply not enough hours in the day to study everything. As great spotted woodpeckers have continued to increase in numbers throughout Ireland, they have now become a more common sight, and are easier to study and observe. As such, I began to dedicate more of my time to following the lives of the other animals that lived along the same river that flowed through those woodpeckers' homeland.

I did not do this with the intention of writing another book, I did it because it is what I enjoy most: being alone in the natural world, watching animals going about their business and seeing moments in their lives witnessed by no one other than myself. I had regularly seen kingfishers along this river while writing my first book; for the most part a brief flash of blue and orange. In the same manner as I had set out to find the woodpeckers' nest, I decided to embark on a search to find the kingfishers' nest site, thinking at the time it would be a straightforward task.

As my study of the woodpeckers began to reveal unexpected developments in their family life, the kingfishers countered by refusing to divulge theirs in any shape or form. Meanwhile, other animals such as dippers, grey wagtails, goosanders and even otters went about their daily business, which to me was just as exciting as the pursuits and activities of the woodpeckers or kingfishers. Clearly this river and its surrounding woodland had a broader story to tell than just that of finding a bird's nest.

As I found myself wanting to spend more time in nature's company, I also found that I needed to do so for my own well-being. It is well known that immersing oneself in nature is a good antidote to the stresses of modern-day life, and I have always felt the pull of the natural world when faced with everyday challenges.

For me, part of studying nature consists of writing observations. In addition to producing a permanent record, I have always found it easier to express myself through writing than speaking. As my sightings and records of the kingfishers grew, they became entangled with the thoughts and moods I escaped to the river with each day. As such, I realized another book had been born, one in which the river would become the main character as it linked the past, the present and flowed into the future.

But although I watched the birds alone, the publication of this book was the culmination of many people's work, support and assistance. I consider myself fortunate to have behind me a publisher who believes not just in me but in my work. The Lilliput Press has been a tower of encouragement and help. Without its amazing staff this book simply would not have been possible. Thank you to Ruth Hallinan, Dana Halliday and Niall McCormack, designer, and a special debt of thanks is due to publisher Antony Farrell for his endless support.

My editor, Djinn von Noorden, is one of the most amazing people I have worked with during the writing of this book. Although she gently guided and corrected my writing and grammar, she nevertheless allowed me the freedom to express myself. She continually encouraged this as it helped convey my personality more clearly. Thank you, Djinn.

I would not have been able to watch many of the birds' lives I followed were it not for the assistance of Paul McGuinness and Kathy Gilfillan. They allowed me unfettered access throughout their property while I followed the lives of the animals that lived in and around the river. Kevin Singleton, their groundsman, also willingly assisted me further in many ways.

Writing this book would not have been possible without the assistance of people far more gifted in literary skills and the art of storytelling than me. Many people helped with ideas and concepts at different stages, most of which are incorporated. However, several people have been so closely involved that they are almost an integral part of the book itself and deserve a special mention.

John Boorman gave me tremendous support and encouragement from the book's conception and initial words to its conclusion. Generous with his time and lavish with his insights, his contributions are scattered throughout the book like autumn leaves floating past on the river itself.

Alan Gilsenan, with his experience in both writing and film production, did a wonderful job in bringing the story together. His suggestions and nuanced contributions at changing direction and controlling moods within the book ensured it flowed smoothly from start to finish.

Niall Hatch quite literally knows every full stop and punctuation mark within these pages. He ensured, throughout my copious early drafts, that punctuation, grammar and spelling were not just adhered to but tactfully explained in the hope of avoiding further transgressions of the English language. The many faux pas and blunders that crept into my writing during its early stages were dealt with in an experienced, relaxed and friendly manner. Always encouraging, his involvement guaranteed the book's completion.

The story of the birds in this book is greatly enhanced by the photographs so generously provided by John Murphy. As a photographer he is skilled in the art of composition and experienced in fieldcraft. As such, his work captures moments that are fleeting and easily missed. It is a privilege to see his expertise bringing many aspects of the story so vividly to life.

The two beautiful full-page illustrations were provided by my friend Clodagh Power. With her amazing talent and understanding of the story's tone, she both set the scene for the story and then expertly caught the atmospheric mood of its later change in direction. I am delighted she was able to make such a valuable contribution to my book.

Of course, no man is an island, no matter how much he may strive to be one. Although most of my observations in this book were made alone, I was fortunate to have a constant mentor with whom to share, discuss and enjoy them afterwards. I am grateful, as always, to my lifelong friend Dick Coombes, not just for his companionship and knowledge, but also for his continuing endurance of my company through the many ups and downs of my life.

The beautifully written and inspiring foreword by Lilly Platt captures, from a young person's perspective, the environment I studied. Lilly is thirteen years old and lives in the Netherlands where she is known for going on peaceful strikes to voice out environmental concerns. She is a global environmentalist, speaker and youth ambassador for the Plastic Pollution Coalition, YouthMundus and World Oceans Day Italy (WODI). Sadly, our beautiful world and its wildlife are in trouble. I believe the safekeeping of our planet lies not so much in my hands, but in the hands of young people.

Lilly, like many other young people, is a climate-striker and has taken to the streets and social media to protest and raise awareness of the damage we are doing. In the past three years she has picked up over 100,000 pieces of plastic and, by her actions, saved countless animals and habitats from being destroyed. Although not living in Ireland, she knows the very river I wrote about and has walked its banks with her grandfather. I am delighted she was able to contribute to my book and would encourage everyone to support her cause by following her on Twitter @lillyspickup.

In as much as a river is like time, it has moods and temperaments that are constantly in flux. Likewise, the writing of this book flowed through a range of ambiances and atmospheres, from elation to despair. As such, I am forever indebted to the support of my family: my brothers, Gerry and Kevin; my sister, Sheila; and sisters-in-law, Patricia and Olive. Their help lay not in the words that I wrote, but in the fact that they were actually written. Without their continuous emotional support, the figurative pen would have been placed down long before the book's conclusion.

My children, Luke and Emily, have been a great source of support and encouragement throughout their lives. I love sharing the natural world with them and seeing that world through their eyes as they express nature's wonder back to me. Moreover, they also show me a world I did not, or could not, see.

For this, and their endless love, thank you.

Finally, I cannot forget a woof of gratitude to my most faithful spotted companion, Lucy. Always beside me, always there for me – and now a pronounced expert on the lives of kingfishers.

And so, the story begins ...

# PROLOGUE:
## PATTERNS IN THE SAND

I SEE PATTERNS in nature all the time: everywhere I look there is order and beauty, overlaid with designs and configurations. They emerge from everything I see, like a flower slowly unfurling its petals in the ethereal, golden light of the first rays of the rising sun.

The clouds overhead: not just a cohesion of water molecules, to be categorized with names such as 'cumulus', 'cirrus', 'altostratus' and 'cumulonimbus', but rather every possible form of nature that can burst forth from my mind. Cirrus clouds become horses' tails, a peacock's tail feather, the feathery plumes of pampas grass.

Tiny grains of sand blowing across, at their scale, the seemingly infinite and empty expanse of a beach: rather than drifting randomly on the draughts, they form lines, shapes and mathematical arrangements, creating order. Constantly changing, the exact mechanism that directs the movement of these tiny particles of stone is still not fully understood. Not that this matters to me. I don't have to understand nature to appreciate it – to do that, I only have to look around me.

I have often been asked what is the best way to watch or appreciate nature. Such a question unnecessarily overcomplicates a simple matter.

We only have to stop and take time to see, to hear and to *feel* the world around us. We need to still the mind and allow it the space and time to explore its surroundings. We need to try to recapture the simple wonder we had when we were younger and saw our first robin or touched our first rabbit.

But, rather than just rediscovering it, we must be brave enough to admit that we want it. Children growing up are actively encouraged to use their imagination by parents and teachers. Why then, when they are older, are they told to stop daydreaming, as though this were unacceptable behaviour?

A flock of birds wheeling, darting and diving in the sky – birds such as starlings, dunlins, knots or golden plovers – all display feats of manoeuvrability and split-second reactions that we supposedly more advanced humans cannot begin to replicate. Yet can they see, or appreciate, the patterns and shapes that their actions create? Or does this ability live only in the human mind?

As I study the birds, animals and plants around me, I cannot help but see the patterns all living things seem driven to create. The riparian world I explored and the rivers I followed while writing this book provided me with so much insight into this aspect of nature. The kingfishers, dippers, goosanders and great spotted woodpeckers that form a central part of this story are as much bound to the patterns of the natural world as those tiny grains of sand blowing across that seemingly empty expanse.

Like the river's rippling currents here alongside me, or the currents of air wafting those 'peacock feathers' overhead, I am as bound to these patterns of nature as they are …

I merely need to open my eyes to see them.

# GENESIS

THE KINGFISHER HAD been sitting quietly on the far side of the river opposite me for quite some time, its patience mirrored by my own stillness and solitude. Occasionally, it bobbed its brightly coloured head up and down or tilted it sideways to look at the water below, but otherwise stillness prevailed.

It knew I was there, or at least I thought it did; sometimes it is hard enough to understand my own thoughts without trying to understand those of another. I continued to watch, and time continued to pass, as did the river that separated us. Possibly the most colourful bird in Ireland, it was all but invisible amongst the riverside foliage.

The vividly coloured plumage, with its multiple shades of blue, orange and white, seemed to pulsate in the dappled shade of the overhead branches. Each feather was like a mathematical fractal: the closer you scrutinized it, the more detail was revealed, spiralling downwards towards infinity. Spots within spots, circles within circles, lines within lines: a never-ending pattern of complexity that could drive you to madness if pursued – and this from only a single feather. The broken light that filtered through the cracks between leaves played, danced and flickered across its small, compact body, breaking up outlines and creating movement where none had existed before.

It was there – it was not there.

In some ways the kingfisher is a strangely proportioned bird, reminiscent of a hobgoblin: its long, pointed bill is far longer than its head and creates a strangely top-heavy appearance. This disproportion is further enhanced by an absurdly short tail that could hardly act as a counterbalance to its weighty front end. Its tiny feet restrict its movements to the occasional sideways shuffle on a suitable branch or post. I sat there, unmoving. This was the bird I had been searching for.

A distance separated us – the bird and the watcher – not simply the width of the river but a vast gulf, stretching back over eons of time. The river beside which I sat had flowed through this valley for thousands of years, but it had not created the valley itself. The glacier that had gouged out this landscape had occurred so far back in time that not even a vestigial inherited memory remained in my head. Part of a mammoth ice sheet, the glacier had encompassed the land for miles, in five different directions. The waters that now rippled past us in its place were but a final act of an ancient play on a giant stage.

This little jewel of the river, perched opposite me, was not a recent arrival. Nor was it a traveller following an ancient pathway to an unknown destination. No, its kind had been here for thousands of years, far longer than the people who had since colonized this land as the ice sheets retreated northwards, driven by warming temperatures and the advancing birch woodlands. Those frozen Arctic behemoths had erased life from thousands of square kilometres, driving the embattled Pleistocene fauna to attempt to forge an existence at the boundary of ice and wood. But the advancing greenwood and life-giving flowing water that began to dominate the emerging landscape brought life to the cold, barren world and provided opportunities where few had existed before.

This wonderful blue-and-orange creation, the kingfisher, was born and shaped by evolution. It had been moulded to fit its environment alongside fabulous landscapes, amidst natural wonders that I could only speculate and dream about. Mammoths, woolly rhinoceroses and sabre-toothed tigers had all coexisted with birds such as this before succumbing, unable to embrace the changing environment – yet, against all these odds, this tiny bird had adapted and succeeded.

I wondered whether a glimmer of those ancient landscapes remained in the inherited memory of this bird: instinct, honed by survival, passed on generation after generation. Not even the size of my fist, and with a brain a quarter the size of my eyeball, there was probably more instinct packed into the cranium of this riverside beauty than existed in my own. My abilities were learned, not inherited.

But rather than merely surviving, the kingfisher had risen to the challenge and is now a common and widespread species in suitable habitats across Europe and Asia. Despite this, it often goes unnoticed, and many people live out their lives without ever experiencing the speechlessness that comes with a first sighting of this true azure beauty. So why was I watching it? Why was I sitting on a grass bank with the growing pangs of cramp extending their painful tendrils up my legs?

Because I was on a quest.

It may sound grandiose – while sitting on a patch of damp grass, staring at a small bird – to declare that this was the reason I was there. But following this bird, as I was doing, meant that I was on a journey of some kind, and usually a purpose accompanies the traveller, though not always. For me, the embodiment of all quests is undeniably King Arthur's Knights of the Round Table searching for the Holy Grail. Yet they did not know what the Holy Grail actually *represented*, but what they saw, what they did and what they experienced *became* the legend: the story of their journey, not the object of their desire.

I had often seen kingfishers while birdwatching, both in Ireland and further afield. However, although I had seen them feeding, fighting and nesting, I would not say that I knew their lives intimately. And certainly not like the family of great spotted woodpeckers I had watched in the nearby wood, and whose lives I had come to share. The complete cycle of birth and death, which I had witnessed amongst the woodpeckers, whose dead chicks I had cradled in my hands, was not one I shared with kingfishers.

Throughout my woodland wanderings in search of woodpeckers, I had followed this river and its tributaries through the wooded valleys of the Wicklow Mountains. I had encountered kingfishers in many areas: small mountain streams, glaciated lakes, steep-sided gorges and tranquil ponds. But, as is often the case with this secretive species, the sightings were brief, unexpected and irregular. Although the great spotted woodpecker has no affiliation with rivers in the manner that a kingfisher does, there was, nonetheless, a link between the two here in Wicklow.

Much, if not all, of the oak wood in the Wicklow Mountains is not primal wood, but rather was planted several hundred years ago following extensive deforestation. Many areas were planted because they were not suitable for farming or cultivation, and these included the many valleys that extend like the fingers on an outstretched hand across the Wicklow Mountains. These valleys became the homes of the first great spotted woodpeckers, which colonized Ireland in 2007. But they were already home to other birds, including the kingfisher.

This world, this planet, our home, is an amazing place. Whether we realize it or not, every living thing is entwined like an intricate web of mycelium in the soil. Unseen, living in darkness, this labyrinth of filaments, like the countless neurons that make up the human brain, forms a net through which chemical messages can travel: a net that extends its threads for miles, linking animals, people, habitats and ultimately ecosystems.

Realizing this, I knew that woodpeckers and other birds could not be studied in isolation, but only in conjunction with the world around them. Because of their different habitat requirements, the great spotted woodpecker and the kingfisher may rarely, if ever, cross paths here in Wicklow. Nevertheless, they share the same environment and often live in close proximity to one another. One location, two different realms. My journey was to enter these worlds, not knowing where it was going to take me nor what I was going to find when I got there.

Although most people may not actually have seen a kingfisher, it is a familiar bird and its appearance is known to most. It commands attention due to its startling colours and its spectacular dives, piercing the surface of the water with its dagger-like bill. Its arresting plumage and distinctive behaviour have long made it a favourite of photographers, artists and filmmakers. However, many of its neighbours who share the same riparian world are complete strangers to all but birdwatchers and naturalists. Birds such as the dipper, goosander and grey wagtail live out equally captivating lives, but often in obscurity.

Despite its apparent familiarity, much of the kingfisher's lifestyle is shrouded in quiet secrecy, performed out of sight and hidden from view. There was knowledge to be found – but this was not a quest for knowledge; this was a journey for something else.

It has often been said that you cannot step into the same river twice. Place your foot in the water, take it out and put it back in again – it is not the same river; the water is different, the very life within it has changed. It is a different river. In the same manner, you can watch the same bird again and again, but each time is a new experience: different light, different sounds, different skies, different temperature … a different experience – a *new* experience.

The pleasure I get from the natural world around me comes from immersing myself in each such experience, regardless of whether I learn something new or not. It comes from deep within me, from enjoying each new moment. All of nature contributes to this experience, although for many people only the prettier aspects of nature capture their attention, like the colours of the kingfisher; but colour is not everything. While kingfishers can captivate people in the briefest of moments, many less extravagant-looking species get ignored. I try to see the magic in every moment and every species we share the planet with; although I admit it can sometimes be hard to sell the merits of the brown rat or tarantula.

Some birds and animals create a memorable moment when first encountered and remain fixed in the mind forever. I clearly remember seeing my first great spotted woodpecker, both in England, when I was visiting as a boy, and more recently in Ireland. But I can also recall my first lizard, when I was only three years old; the first time I identified greenfinches at the age of seven; and my first frog only a year or so later. But I do not remember my first snail or woodlouse (though I *do* remember my first centipede, as did my mother!). So, some stories, and journeys, do have a specific starting point, whereas others do not ...

But the beginning of this journey did not begin with an event, or a bird, or an ambition – it began many years ago with a colour, and that colour was ... blue.

# THE SOURCE

BLUE WAS WHAT I remembered most that day, that and my father ...

A lazy, slow-moving river flowed alongside us as we walked along a quiet laneway in County Wexford, coming from nowhere in particular and going to the same place. It was mid-afternoon, the weather was fine and the world was fresh. It was Easter, I was nine years old and we were on holiday. I was bursting with excitement, with anticipation and expectation, while my father was merely glad the long journey was over.

Coming from Dublin, Wexford was a different world, not just a different county. Back then, there were no motorways or bypasses by which to travel to the south-eastern corner of Ireland. There was just the N11 that meandered, in wide, arcing loops like a river, across the eastern province, resulting in a three-hour journey to travel the 170 kilometres to our destination. We came to County Wexford for our holidays every year, and often to different parts. We came because of me.

We lived in the suburbs of Dublin, in Blackrock, and I hated it – not because it was a horrible place to live but because for a young naturalist like me it was stifling and barren. I wanted space to roam, air to breathe and most of all quietness to watch birds and animals. I wanted the countryside. This might sound like an unusual yearning for a young boy growing up in suburbia – after all, Dublin had so much to offer people of all ages and catered for a huge variety of interests. Facilities abounded – playgrounds, youth clubs, cinemas, sports halls and playing fields. However, Dublin failed to cater properly for me, because I had only one interest in my young life, and that was the natural world.

For as long as I could remember, I had had no interest other than nature. Mammals, amphibians, reptiles, flowers, insects and especially birds filled my every waking minute, leaving little room in my developing brain for much else. Other children my age had interests that were more 'normal': football, rugby, tennis, swimming, summer camps, scouts and a host of other activities. As for me?

Sports completely eluded me. I could not understand the point, the rules or the purpose. Rugby, football, GAA – they were all the same, simply something I could not relate to. It was hard enough for me to understand, let alone remember, the rules – and as for the purpose? Well, that involved teamwork and communication; and that certainly did not come naturally to me.

Summer camps meant having things in common with other children and developing new talents, and I had yet to find anyone who wanted to talk about the life of an earwig or share the excitement of keeping tadpoles in the bedroom. Anyway, why did I need new talents other than expanding my knowledge of the wonderful, if sometimes incomprehensible, world around me?

Today we accept and expect instant communication and connectivity. The answer to a question is often only a few strokes of a keyboard or stabs on a smartphone screen away. But when I was a young boy growing up, this 'luxury' had barely been conceived, let alone implemented. Seeking answers, I endlessly reread my numerous wildlife books, the number of which grew at an extraordinary and exponential rate. Christmas and birthdays provided further opportunities to expand my resources: binoculars, microscopes, magnifying glasses, books on flowers, on animals, on birds, on trees, on beetles, on bees ... the list was never-ending.

Although I was, and still am, interested in all aspects of nature, birds held a special interest for me. Even at a young age, they fascinated me more than anything else, with their intricately plumaged bodies, their myriad colours and their ability to fly. Our Blackrock garden, thanks to the diligent attention of my father, was a sanctuary of trees, shrubs and flowers. Like an oasis in a suburban desert, birds fed, bathed and nested there. I spent hours staring out my bedroom window, watching magpies building their nests or greenfinches quarrelling over the birdseed on the bird table my brother Gerry had built for me.

Although my parents and older siblings did not share my passion with the same intensity, they affectionately indulged and nurtured my interest in birds. The bird table, built by my father from scraps of old wood, was a case in point. Scraps were saved from the Sunday dinner and monkey nuts were laboriously threaded onto a length of cotton thread by my mother while she watched television. And the birds repaid our combined efforts with hours of antics and amusement. Greenfinches, chaffinches, bullfinches, house sparrows, starlings, robins, blackbirds ... I could barely keep pace with my *Spotter's Guide to Birds*, the definitive reference book at the time. As I looked through my parents' 4x20 opera glasses, I struggled, alone, to learn the differences contained within the squabbling flocks outside our kitchen window. The fast-moving birds in the small binoculars rarely matched the colourful, little paintings in the books.

Perhaps surprisingly, my fascination with nature was not something I 'picked up' from my parents, older brothers or sister. Certainly, my parents enjoyed going for walks; however, they were unaware of most names of the innumerable wonders we passed during our weekend rambles. But they recognized my interest, my need and in some ways my differences. While they may well have felt it strange, even odd, they facilitated me as much as they could, as indeed did all my family.

While my older brothers, Gerry, Kevin and Brian, were not as captivated by animals as I was, they certainly were not averse to them. Like many children they kept various pets, which only focused my interest ever more away from any social activities, as there were always animals to occupy my mind. Even from a very young age, my family often let me have my way wherever animals were concerned. One morning, when I was only three years old, my eldest brother Gerry was trying to choose a name for his new grey rabbit, one of several he kept in a large outdoor pen named 'The Warren'. I was sitting on the grass nearby and had no sooner seen his armful of grey fluff when I began shouting, 'Me! Me! Me!' The rabbit was subsequently named Meme, effectively to humour me. I was extremely fortunate, and still am, to have such a caring family.

Rabbits, guinea pigs, mice, gerbils, budgerigars, zebra finches – my brothers had them all, as did I, but I later added terrapins; hedgehogs; frogs; newts; snails; caterpillars; a sea aquarium filled with prawns, crabs, starfish and baby lobsters; and countless injured birds. The list of bird casualties was sadly a long one: chaffinches, robins, house sparrows, blackbirds, dunnocks, starlings – even a young herring gull we named Fred.

Fred lived with us for almost a year, having been found badly injured on a beach by my brother Brian. A sympathetic local vet had saved his life and released him into our care. However, it had necessitated amputating both a leg and a wing, and we spent many months nursing him back to health in the hope he could be rehomed to a zoo or local wildlife sanctuary. Fred spent every night safely inside a large hut built especially for him by my father, with help from Gerry. During the day he would hop around the garden, exploring the symmetrically coloured flowerbeds and manicured lawns, which were lovingly cared for by Dad. Sometimes Fred would tilt his head and look longingly – and forlornly, to my eyes – skyward as other gulls soared and flapped overhead. Every now then he would give a plaintive and lonesome wheezing call, so characteristic of young herring gulls, but it always went unheeded. As I lay on the grass, my head propped on my hands, I empathized with his loneliness.

Fred appeared to thrive on what I now know to be a highly unsuitable diet of whatever was left over in the kitchen. Wretchedly, ten months later, we found his still-warm body lying amongst the swathes of nodding daffodils. Sadly, like so many of the other waifs and strays I rescued, I was unable to provide the expert care that he needed. Fred was one of many, and most of them died, despite my best efforts to care for them – something I never learned to cope with, and perhaps never will, and which left me in tears for days.

In time, my siblings' interests matured from rabbits to various sports, social activities and relationships. My own obsession failed to wane, on the other hand, and my long-suffering parents continued to endure frogs in the bedroom for many years to come. I became more and more absorbed in the natural world around me, withdrawing into it … immersing myself in it. But a garden, some manicured parks and regular Sunday afternoon walks were not enough to satisfy my need. With nothing else to occupy me, and with no one else of similar age around to share my interest, the summer holidays were a prolonged struggle, especially for my parents.

In an effort to keep me happy, each year – and sometimes twice a year, during the summer and at Easter – my parents took me, and occasionally one or two of my siblings, to the countryside for a holiday. And so, walking along a river with my father, going nowhere in particular, looking at every butterfly, bird, flower and ladybird I spotted with my eager child's eyes did not feel unusual – not for me, anyway.

Many of our summer holiday destinations were located close to a beach. There my parents could relax in the sunshine while I explored the tideline for exciting, new discoveries. During the Easter holidays, if we did go away then, it was not to the beach but to more pastoral locations, some of which were alongside a river.

One particular Easter, my father and I were walking along the river close to our rented holiday home. The river was nearing the end of its journey and, while not tidal, was close to expanding into an estuary. It was late April, and the lane we walked along was verdant with emergent growth. Alexanders, a relative of cow parsley, flourished on both the riverbank and underneath the ancient hedgerow on the opposite side of the lane. Half-hidden under their glossy, piquant, camphor-scented foliage were a host of other spring and early-summer flowers: primroses, Jack-by-the-hedge, ramsons, dog violets, lords-and-ladies and so many others, all of whose names I knew from my books. Old, gnarled and twisted hawthorns were the dominant species of tree in this hedgerow. Their buds were bursting into leaf, covering the skeletal mass of branches in what looked like fine, pale-green gauze. In the coming weeks they would be covered in masses of white flowers, like the heaps of frothy, white foam that slowly spiralled and swirled around in the river beside us.

While my father walked quietly in his steady, determined manner, I spent the time running from one wonder to the next. Each new discovery brought endless questions, all of which I happily heaped upon him. He did his best to help his youngest child with his unusual interests, but so many of these discoveries were new to him as well. Usually, the most he could do was to share the wonder with me, and often that was enough.

A bird called nearby and a pair of small birds, their bodies as round and fuzzy as cotton-wool balls, flew across the track, trailing tails that were more than twice as long as their bodies. My father, fortunately and amazingly, recognized them, for I had never seen anything like them before: a pair of long-tailed tits. Restless, always moving and rarely seen alone, for many people they are the least familiar of the tit family. I had never encountered them before or seen them visiting our suburban garden, since they are a woodland species.

They continued to forage amongst the emergent hawthorn leaves, calling incessantly, seemingly oblivious to my presence. Predominantly white, they had a black stripe on each side of their heads and another across their wings. The white feathers on their backs were suffused with pink, making them look like partially chocolate-covered marshmallows. However, it was those tails – oh, those tails – that were the crowning glory of these feathered woodland sprites. Longer than their bodies, they seemed completely out of proportion, yet perfectly balanced the coloured golf balls attached to them. I was thrilled: our first day and our holiday was already introducing me to exciting, new creatures. My diary would be busy trying to keep up with my racing, overactive mind.

Once the birds had disappeared, we carried on down the laneway. It became more unmanaged and overgrown as we progressed, the centre of the track increasingly green as grasses and spring flowers turned it into a linear meadow. The encroaching wildness was grist to my mill, bringing me further into the natural world I so desperately sought. After a period, this verdant channel turned right and crossed the river by means of a centuries-old bridge.

We stood alone in this ethereal, green paradise, my father and I, looking across the bridge to the other side. It was a magical bridge, which felt like it belonged to a different world – a world where King Arthur and his knights rode forth on their quest for the Holy Grail. The bridge had been built many centuries earlier when the ruined Franciscan abbey that towered in the distant fields was at its height as a place of solitude, prayer and learning. The sides of the bridge were higher than my head and were crowned with rectangular blocks spaced at regular intervals. It looked like the top of an Arthurian castle had been dropped in front of us.

However, it was not just the sight of the bridge that arrested our progress: there was something else on that bridge, something orangey-red. A fox sat there with his back to us, his russet fur glowing in the evening sunshine. Although its correct name is a red fox, its pelt is not actually red. Its orange coat was in stark contrast to the vibrant spring grass on which it sat. I stared in complete disbelief at the animal in front of me. It was my first ever sighting of a fox.

When I was growing up, foxes were not a common sight in the Dublin suburbs or even in the city itself. Today, in contrast, they are often seen in daylight, strolling across gardens or sleeping in flowerbeds, completely indifferent to people. Their adaption to suburban living was proven beyond doubt recently when one morning my brother Gerry opened his back door: there was a loud thump and a surprised 'yip' as he knocked a sleeping fox off the doorstep!

However, that suburban fox of the future was far removed from this wily, rural resident. We stood in silence. No sounds, other than the slow gurgling and burbling of the river around us, disturbed that moment. After what felt like an eternity, the fox roused itself from its reverie and stood up. Without even a backward glance, it walked along the bridge until reaching the end, where it briefly turned around to look at us before slipping quietly into the hedgerow's tangled undergrowth.

A pair of long-tailed tits and a fox hardly seem pivotal events, and perhaps to many other children they would appear inconsequential ... but not to me. Both species were beyond my wildest dreams at that time. They represented the opposite of the suburban habitat where I lived. They occupied a different dominion, a seemingly unattainable world – a world I ached to explore.

I bombarded my father with questions about our new, bushy-tailed acquaintance. Why was it there? Where was it going? Where did it live? What did it eat? And so on. My father, unable to answer his son's endless interrogation, just smiled, and we walked on across the bridge. The high walls and battlements on the bridge, those rectangular blocks with their corresponding notched spacings, meant I was unable to see the river below. My father lifted me up and I could see the full expanse of the river below for the first time ... supported by him, I discovered a new world.

It was not an enormous watercourse, by any standard, or one that had traversed the length of the country: it was a small river of little significance. In the distant hills of north Wexford, two smaller tributaries had emerged and flowed south through the rolling farmland and open countryside. They had converged further north of this place to create the riparian environment that now lay below me.

The estuary in the distance marked the end of one world and the start of a completely new and novel habitat. From the moment the first drops of water trickled out of the ground, they had been compelled to travel to the sea to meet their destiny. Drawn in a manner akin to the one in which a swallow is compelled to fly south, drawn by forces beyond its control.

The river was at it its broadest at this point and was slow-flowing, having expended its turbulent force and erosive power further upstream. The banks were ill-defined, a merging of water and lush vegetation in various stages of growth and levels of density.

The final division between land and water was further blurred by the proliferation of floating plants that extended outward from the rushes, reeds and waterside herbage. Water crowfoot, water bistort and watercress all grew in proliferation. Willow trees leaned out from the bank, extending their limbs out beyond the waterside foliage and dangling their furthest leaves into the water below. The currents rippling past the dipping leaf tips created swirling patterns and shapes as elusive and insubstantial as smoke. The images I saw for each split-second were created by physics but given life by the power of my imagination. I wished I could have perched on those branches like a bird and watched the river from that perspective. No, not *like* a bird. I wished I could have *been* a bird.

There were other birds there too: species with which I was familiar from the suburban parks – unlike those feathered marshmallows, the long-tailed tits. Dumpy-looking moorhens, sometimes called water hens, waddled along the banks like small, black chickens. Their bright, yellow-and-red bills were as shiny as melted candle wax. Colourful grey wagtails flitted from stone to stone like little ballerinas, their long tails constantly in motion as they danced and pranced above the water. With their sulphur-yellow underparts and glossy, black throats, they were anything but grey; but it was the soft, blue-grey plumage on their backs which gave them their name. Mallards dabbled in the shallows, close to the edge of the reeds and further downstream, and towards the estuary a grey heron stood motionless in the water. Overwhelmed by so much to look at, so many colours, so much life, so much everything, I did not hear it at first.

A loud, strident whistle sounded from the far side of the bridge. Again it called, a piercing cry that cut through all other sounds, including that of the river itself.

'What was that?' I asked my father.

'I don't know,' he replied.

Again it sounded, as though from the river itself, and now it seemed closer – below us, in fact. I leaned further over the bridge, still anchored by my father, and a bullet of blue sped out from underneath

# THE FISHER KING

IT NEVER CEASES to amaze me that many people are unfamiliar with common birds such as the dipper and grey wagtail. They are not rare or unusual; they stay in Ireland all year around, yet they remain unknown. People look at them but do not see them until their eyes are opened. However, the kingfisher suffers no such fate.

Its vivid palette of blues and oranges raises it to a level far above 'little brown birds' or crows. Its habit of feeding, by diving like an arrow into the water, is unique in Ireland and captures people's attention, regardless of their level of interest in the nature around them. Because it is the only member of the kingfisher family in Ireland, it is usually called simply the 'kingfisher'. Sometimes it is referred to by other names, which do not feature in most common bird books or field guides, such as 'river kingfisher', 'European kingfisher' and 'common kingfisher'. This is to separate it from its fellow family members, many of which live in open, dry countryside far from water of any kind. However, one of the names by which I knew it from my youth was different to any of these: 'Halcyon'.

'Halcyon days' conjures up images of calm and peace – rarely do people associate it with birds, especially kingfishers. Although the term is associated with the long, pleasant days of summer and youth, the origin of the phrase is set in the depths of winter, and the true halcyon days take place during the darkest time of the year.

According to a Greek myth recorded by Ovid, a Roman poet living at the time of Christ, the halcyon was a bird. Although not stated as a fact, it was generally considered to refer to the bird we now know as the kingfisher. As with many aspects of mythology, the legend of the kingfisher, or halcyon, varies depending on the storyteller ...

Aeolus was the keeper of the winds and king of the mythical floating island of Aeolia. His power to control the violent storm winds was entrusted to him by Zeus, king of the gods. The daughter of Aeolus was named Alcyone, and she married Ceyx. Living together happily on a beach, the couple saw themselves as comparable to the Olympian gods, a challenge which enraged Zeus. Furious at their disrespect, he turned them both into birds: Ceyx into a vulture and his wife into a seabird named Halcyon.

Unlike other birds, many of which migrated during the autumn – a phenomenon not properly understood at the time by the Greek writers – Halcyon stayed all year round and laid her eggs in the depths of winter. She made a nest of fishbones and located it in a crevice in the rocks. However, each time the strong winds and waves would wash away the eggs before they hatched, or the chicks before they had learnt to fly. The gods of Olympus were so moved by Halcyon's heartbreaking cries of despair for her young that they granted a period of fourteen days of good weather during late December and early January. During this time the winds were light, the seas were calm and the sun shone, allowing Halcyon to brood her eggs and teach the chicks to fly without being swept away by the waves.

Traditionally, the fourteen days were set around the winter solstice, an important date in legend and mythology. Halcyon built her nest during the seven days before the year's shortest day and hatched her young during the subsequent seven days. However, some other accounts of the mythical event hold that the halcyon days occur in January.

Although Wicklow is a considerable distance from the Aegean Sea, where Halcyon brooded her young, I find it fascinating that, two thousand years after this account was written, we often do get a period of fine, calm weather for a couple of days in early January. However, it rarely lasts for fourteen days, and I have yet to find any birds nesting – kingfishers or otherwise – at this time of year.

As kingdoms rose and fell, the story of Halcyon, and the gods who ruled her, was pushed aside and forgotten. However, Alcyone, who became Halcyon, will always be remembered by those who can read the stars. The brightest star in the star cluster Pleiades, located in the constellation of Taurus, sometimes referred to as the Seven Sisters, is named after her: Alcyone – the kingfisher star. It is fitting that this star reaches its highest point in the northern hemisphere's southern night sky during midwinter. She shines brightest during those calm, peaceful nights of midwinter, the halcyon days and nights.

The kingfisher is the only member of its family to live in Ireland. It belongs to a family of birds called Alcedinidae, which is part of the Coraciiformes order that includes other colourful birds such as bee-eaters, rollers and the curiously named motmots. The kingfishers are a small- to medium-sized group of birds. They inhabit a widely diverse range of habitats, despite appearing similar in their overall structure and adaptions.

They are a cosmopolitan family, occurring on every continent except Antarctica. Over a period of years, during my travels in search of birds in other countries and in different regions, I have been fortunate enough to see several species of kingfisher, some similar to those we encounter here in Ireland and others widely different.

The pygmy kingfisher from sub-Saharan Africa is the smallest and lives in woodlands. The cutest and most endearing member of this family, the memory of that first encounter is forever etched into my mind's eye, enabling me to relive the moment whenever I so wish. I was in the Gambia, on the west coast of Africa, and making my way through a dense patch of woodland. This habitat differed significantly from any wooded habitat I had encountered in Ireland.

There were no paths, and the ground was dry and arid, while the overhead closed canopy of foliage prevented much of the light from reaching the understory through which we blazed our trail. The ground cover was often sparse, but wherever there was water, no matter how shallow or puddle-like, there were prolific stands of bamboo-like plants. Small ponds were located deep in the undergrowth, providing abundant insect life, which in turn lured in numerous birds.

Hidden amongst the pale, straw-coloured stems was a tiny bird, no bigger than a wren, with orange underparts, a blood-red bill and light-blue upper parts. It fed not by diving into water, but by dropping onto the dry, sandy soil and catching small crickets and other insects. The bright African sunshine and the intermittent patches of dense canopy created a mosaic of contrasting light and dark through which the tiny jewel appeared and disappeared, as though by the wave of a magician's hand.

As well as being home to the smallest of the kingfishers, the Gambia also plays hosts to the largest – the giant kingfisher. Far removed from its tiny cousin, this bird can only be described, albeit fondly, as a brute. Larger than a woodpigeon, there is nothing delicate about its commandeering presence. It has a dark-green, speckled head, which sports a spiky crest and a huge, black bill like a pointed machete. The upper parts are a mixture of greens, greys and black, while its orange, speckled throat forms a collar against its white underparts. Unlike the clear and melodic whistling tones of our kingfisher, this Goliath has a raucous and aggressive, rattling cry.

Many other species of kingfisher also live in the Gambia. Pied kingfishers, with striking black-and-white plumage, hover over the sea in harbours and estuaries. Malachite kingfishers, only marginally larger than the pygmy kingfisher, hide in pondside vegetation, chasing small frogs and fish. Five-star hotel grounds and golf courses often have blue-winged kingfishers sheltering in the elegant palm trees. Preying on lizards, small skinks and geckos, they have adapted well to their man-made environment.

But despite the prolificity of kingfishers in this small country, most are unknown to the general public. The best-known member of the kingfisher family, other than our own, comes from a very different country, where it is not even called a kingfisher. Its mocking call has earned it nicknames such as 'laughing jackass' or 'ha-ha pigeon', while its self-assured demeanour ensured more colloquial titles such as 'Jacky'. Water for this bird is a luxury.

The midday summer heat in the dry eucalyptus woodlands of western Australia can border on unbearable. Every drop of moisture seems to have been sucked out from the land and from the air. This is the terrain of the laughing kookaburra, one of Australia's most iconic birds, known worldwide for its manic, taunting call. This member of the kingfisher family has no affiliation to water, living its life in open, wooded countryside. Towering gum trees, mallee scrub and heat-shimmering Dryandra brushland shelter the countless snakes and lizards on which it feeds. Sitting motionless on a branch, the kookaburra quickly drops onto an unsuspecting reptile and batters it to death by holding it in its bill and smacking the unfortunate animal sharply off the ground.

Although the kingfisher favours rivers in Ireland, it also occurs on lakes and reservoirs. After the breeding season is finished, it can often be seen at coastal harbours and estuaries during the winter months. It is a small bird, about the size of a robin, and squat in appearance. Its dumpy shape creates the impression that it has no neck and is just a colourful ball with a dagger at the front, namely its beak. And what a beak: almost a third of its total length, it is a stunning feature on such a small bird. Long, pointed and perfectly streamlined, it turns this small, rotund bird into the avian equivalent of an Exocet missile or an F-22 jet fighter, as it cleanly and sharply pierces the water surface.

The kingfisher feeds solely on submerged prey, which they catch by diving from a height into the water and grasping the prey, not spearing it, before re-emerging in an explosion of shiny water droplets. It usually hunts from an overhanging perch such as a branch, but in the absence of this it will hover above the water surface before closing its wings and slicing into the watery world below it. Like a kestrel, hanging in the wind above a field watching for prey, the kingfisher scans the river for the slightest movement that might betray its quarry.

Viewed in isolation, this act of diving into the water often appears less impressive than it is. Sitting on its perch, or hovering above the water's surface, the kingfisher spots its prey – but before diving, it must calculate its true position. As any secondary-school student of physics will know, light is bent, or refracted, as it travels through water. If the kingfisher were to dive following a line-of-sight trajectory, it would miss its target by a considerable margin.

Many tribal hunters, fishing with spears and harpoons, are also fully aware of this. Mentally calculating the angle of refraction, they thrust their spear where the fish does not appear to be. Underwater, the spear appears from a different angle and strikes the target: success. Two totally different species, one supposedly far more advanced than the other, making the same calculation with the same measure of success. Despite the gulf that separates us, we may have more in common than we think.

During the dive, the kingfisher closes its wings just prior to slicing through the water surface. It relies on its momentum to cover the final distance to its prey. As well as having calculated the angle at which to enter the water, it will have calculated the speed at which to conduct the dive. Too fast and it could strike the bottom; too slow and it may fail to reach its intended victim. Its eyes remain closed for the duration of its submergence, the feat of snatching its quarry carried out blindly, based on mental calculations of distance, direction and speed.

While the initial dive into the water has become, for many, the iconic image of this spectacular bird, it is the completion of the task that captivates me. Having momentarily disappeared from view, submerged in the source of all life, it explodes upwards from the still-cascading fountain of water droplets. Like a phoenix being reborn, it emerges bill first, its wings pushing it from one realm to another through a membrane of shattered silver. Grasping its struggling, slippery trophy, it lands on its perch, having completed the mundane task of fetching dinner. Sometimes, looking at nature is not the same as seeing it for what it truly is: a wonderful culmination of something we are all part of, a shared heritage, a wondrous web of intricately linked forms. And an experience not to be ignored.

The coffee-coloured rivers of the Wicklow Mountains, covered in swathes of white foam as they rollick over the rocks of the glaciated valleys, are as much home to this brightly coloured jewel as the lazy, meandering and tranquil depths of the lowlands. Although they can often be seen along the banks of lakes and reservoirs, they seem not to favour these as much during the breeding season, possibly due to their prey being less concentrated and more widely dispersed than on a river.

Kingfishers do not completely abandon the upland rivers during the winter months, unlike, say, swallows, which bid the nearby farm buildings a farewell until the spring. Quite often during early winter, river levels do not greatly fluctuate or freeze over. Kingfishers then remain in the area, roaming over many kilometres of river, with no loyalty to any given stretch. But, inevitably and predictably, the winter will tighten its grasp on nature. By the time the winter solstice dawns and the first shafts of its golden light reach out over the bare branches of the silent, sleeping oak woods, many kingfishers will have ventured downstream to the rich coastal feeding grounds. During those midwinter months when they arrive at the coast, they can be seen in saltmarshes, harbours and estuaries. Because the water rarely freezes there, they can feed at their leisure on their favoured prey, the common prawn.

It is often easier to watch kingfishers in the winter months when they visit the coast than during the summer on their riverside breeding grounds. There, despite being brightly coloured, they often sit unobtrusively under the overhanging waterside herbage and blend in with the dappled foliage. But on their coastal wintering grounds there is no such problem with frustrating, half-hidden views. They might happily sit, completely exposed, on a fencepost along the edge of an estuary, resplendent in all their glory, to the delight of those lucky observers who are fortunate enough to see them.

It was early January, and therefore quite likely one of the halcyon days – depending on which mythology you read – when I began looking for my local kingfishers in earnest. There was no logic, rhyme or reason to this commencement date, other than that it was the turning of a year. Birdwatchers and naturalists are often fascinated with dates: the first bird sighting of the year, the first snowdrop, the last swallow to leave for Africa. Lists and dates are a practice ignored by some and relished by others; but recording my nature observations in a diary was something I had been doing since I was nine. The lifecycle of a kingfisher was certainly not tied to the start of January, nor was that of any other Irish bird that I knew. Picking a starting date and a starting point was just for my own benefit, a way to say that I had begun. But what exactly had I begun, and why?

I had, at a very basic level, begun a search for something. To journey towards a distant goal, to travel to an unknown land or a specific target is, in legend, to launch on a quest. I was by no means comparing my waterside and woodland wanderings to the voyages of Columbus or the adventures of Odysseus, but yes, as always, I was travelling through unknown country – unknown in more ways than many people might comprehend.

The preceding few years had seen me following the adventures of great spotted woodpeckers, and before that I followed the exploits of the humble fox. Farther back, as a boy, I used to follow my cat, Tiger, around the garden, carrying a map and marking down where he went and what he did. The poor animal was most perplexed to see me trailing behind him through the hedges, flowerbeds and even across the neighbours' gardens. The neighbours, on the other hand, were well-used to me appearing unannounced, in pursuit of a frog or grasshopper across their lawns.

To my family's amusement, I reached the conclusion that Tiger had three favourite sunning spots and spent an awful lot of time sleeping in the sun. I even produced detailed maps of the garden, showing the routes he had taken as he tried his best to evade my stealthy surveillance. I doubt whether I discovered anything new about domestic feline behaviour, but, if nothing else, it kept me occupied and outside for an entire day.

Of course, watching birds, especially as an adult, is probably easier for most people to comprehend than following a cat around a suburban garden ... yet the same dilemma arose in my mind. Despite watching kingfishers for many years, I had come to realize that although I had watched them, I hadn't really *see* them. And that problem still applies to so much of the world around me on a daily basis. I see my faithful dog, a Dalmatian, every day – she is rarely more than a few metres from my side – yet I could not draw an accurate map of the many black spots that decorate her beautiful, ivory coat. We look, but we do not *see*; what's more, we notice but often do not remember.

I'm not blessed with a gifted memory, and since childhood have written down everything I notice in the natural world, be it important, relevant or not. It is simply the way my mind works. By the time I was nine, these random notes had coalesced – at any early age, it has to be said – and become structured into the handwritten nature diaries I still have today.

If I saw a blackbird on a Tuesday at 8.30 am, I wrote that in, along with everything else:

**Sunday, 1 May 1983**
I saw a female blackbird on the back-garden lawn today carrying food. Male sitting in hawthorn tree. It was raining and getting dark …

**Wednesday, 11 May 1983**
Saw my first swallow of the year this afternoon on the way back home from school …
The tadpoles in the aquarium have started growing back legs as well as changing colour from black to brown and spotty. They are starting to turn into 'froglets'!

I can still see those blackbirds, and I remember that evening. It was wet – not very heavy rain, more like a constant drizzle – and I was in my bedroom staring out the window. Our family home is still there, as is my bedroom, and the lawn and flowerbeds still follow the same sweeping contours and meanderings laid out by my dad a lifetime ago. The young boy is gone. Or is he?

If life is a river, then an enormous volume of water has surged beneath the bridge that spans mine. It is unlikely that a single cell of that child now remains on this earth, yet the image was clear, as was the physical account of a relatively unnoteworthy event. But the curiosity and determination that drove me to watch, record and draw everything I saw is as strong today as it was then. A child's perspective, and perhaps attitude, still remains in me, long after that boy left his bedroom.

I am grateful for that, to have that simplistic wonder, appreciation and drive that so many people lack or seem unable to comprehend. I wouldn't want to be without it. It may bring challenges, such as black-and-white thinking, which can lead to further complications, such as anxiety. But the rewards of being literally brought to a sudden halt by the overpowering scent of a flower, or being rendered speechless by the unfathomable beauty of a distant nebula in space? Those rewards make life worth living and endow a person with the strength to rise above its many challenges.

Although January felt like a logical starting date for a study of kingfishers, being the start of a calendar year, it wasn't necessarily an ideal time of year to actually see the birds along this river. Despite this, I decided to walk along a stretch of the river where I had seen kingfishers in the past, but it was not an area I regularly visited due to the dense undergrowth along the banks. During the summer, the almost impenetrable jungle of chest-high bracken and brambles completely obscured any traces of a path. Previous sightings of kingfishers here had been limited to the briefest of flight views, accompanied by my noisy, sweaty and cumbersome progress through that riverside jungle. But that was in the summer. Now, in the depths of winter, the lush growth had been replaced with flattened mats of decaying mahogany- and amber-coloured vegetation.

From beneath this blanket of colour rose the scent of the sleeping winter earth: rich, tangible and fruit-like, it filled the air, and I could taste its primordial scent as I inhaled and filled my lungs with this, nature's elixir. A coating of frosted oaken leaf litter lay on the soil, like delicate creations of lace. The aromas that arose from the humus-rich ground below were complicated with sharp, acrid notes that persisted long after the initial sweetness was spent. An indulgence for the senses, lying at our feet.

I had thought I was alone, except for the world around me, but a movement caught my eye. What I thought was the twisted stump of a tree, its broken boughs and limbs silhouetted against the golden-yellow horizon, streaked with the palest of blue, began to move. A natural sculpture in the form of a broken tree stump suddenly metamorphosed into a human.

The bank of the river on which the angler emerged was white with frost: mounds of dead bracken and briars, flattened by the winter's rain, lay hidden under a veneer of ice. He stood in silhouette against that cold, pastel-coloured sky, as unmoving and contrasting as the trees on either side of him. After a week of storms, the previously leaden skies had cleared and were now a breathtaking canvas I could not take my eyes off. The late-winter sun was low – its zenith scarcely cleared the bare oak trees behind the solitary figure holding a rod.

River fishing was not something I associated with January. I sometimes saw fly-fishers here during the summer, but that was not a winter pastime. Pike, those prehistoric-looking denizens of weedy underwater jungles, are traditionally hunted during December and January. But this was not pike habitat: this was a mountain river engorged by run-off from the surrounding mountains, a fast-flowing torrent strewn with rocks. Pike favour slow-moving, deep water where their mottled colouration makes them invisible amongst the forests of swaying waterweed.

As I watched that human form standing proudly on the bank, an image of the Fisher King came to my ever-wandering mind. This solitary figure in front of me was also king of his domain and like me was on a quest. The irony of this moment was not wasted on me, for the kingfisher and the legend of the Fisher King are intertwined, as are many things in this world.

In Arthurian legend, the Fisher King is a lonesome figure, responsible for the final stages of the quest for the Holy Grail. His given title is the reverse of kingfisher because he too fishes alone, a solitary figure hunting in the realm of water, in the same manner as the brightly coloured bird I now sought. He is unable to join the quest because he is wounded, and he waits quietly and patiently for those on a journey to come by. The river is life and passes him by; human measurement has no meaning on this quest, only time has meaning. Patiently, like a kingfisher, he awaits the river to bring him those on a quest. Like that Spirit of the River, emerging and being reborn from the life-giving waters, the questing knights emerge from the timeless river and approach the Fisher King to ask the question about that which they seek – the Holy Grail. Perhaps, like them, I needed to do the same?

'Good morning,' I called across the gulf that separated us.

'It's a cold one, isn't it?' came the reply.

Obviously, the Fisher King didn't reveal the answer unless the right question was posed. We exchanged pleasantries and I enquired as to whether he had seen kingfishers recently. While he had sporadically encountered them during the summer months, his sightings during the winter were as barren as the kingdom he ruled. He wished me well in my search, as he probably wished all passers-by, and I continued following the river to where it might bring me.

To be honest, I didn't expect to see a kingfisher that day, and in that I was not disappointed. What I really wanted to do was to check the suitability of the riverbanks for breeding kingfishers when, and if, they took up their residence on the river later, in the spring. Studying any animal, including birds, is not just about looking at it and saying to yourself that you've seen it and moving on. It is about learning to see the world through their eyes and senses, and trying to understand how they perceive the wonderful world we share.

I knew from experience what type of habitat kingfishers liked to breed in and frequent, although that experience was far from infallible. The initial stretch of river I walked was not suitable: the water roared, tumbled, frothed and foamed as it crashed over rocks and through mini-gorges, compelled by a chaotic riverscape of boulders, rocks and stones. The surface was constantly in furious motion, regardless of the time of year. It offered no window into the aquatic world below, which held the kingfisher's prey. The almost impenetrable, dense undergrowth extended from the bank where I hacked a path into and below the river. There was no exposed bank face for the kingfisher to burrow into and make its nest.

As I made my way further along the river, a high-pitched series of notes caught my attention: *seeda-seeda-seeda-seeda-see-see-see*. A tiny movement: and a bird, smaller than a mouse, flitted across my vision. A goldcrest, Ireland's smallest bird, was foraging in the bare branches of an alder tree overhanging the water. Smaller than the wren, which is often mistakenly thought of as our smallest bird, this tiny, mossy-green bundle of feathers weighed less than five grams.

It has always amazed me how goldcrests manage to survive the harshness of the winter months, when their food, small invertebrates and spiders, is so hard to come by. Partially silhouetted against the river, it flitted and hovered alongside the ivy leaves that covered the boughs of the tree, gleaning small flies and gnats. The leaves dwarfed its fragile-looking body, and even against the river its two-tone colour was evident.

Its underparts were a pale, off-white colour, similar to the crusty, grey lichens on the trunks of the surrounding oak trees, while its upper parts were the same shade of green as the moss that covered the boulder upon which I sat. Like a hyperactive child, it darted, dipped and foraged in the gloom of the ivy. Despite my proximity to it, I was unable to see the streak of yellowish orange on its crown that gave the bird its name. Moments later it flew off, calling *see-see-see* as it disappeared into the trees.

As I began to put distance between myself and the fisherman, the undergrowth gradually thinned, and I was now able to walk along the bank with a clear view. The water had also changed, and the mood of the river had mellowed. It was deeper, slower-flowing, and the surface was smoother and less disturbed. Clay banks, created by erosion and deposition from the meandering water, emerged along the bends – we were in kingfisher habitat. The banks were not high, about half a metre, but I knew that later in the season, as the water levels dropped to their summer level, more of the clay face would be exposed.

Despite exploring almost a kilometre of river, I had not met a kingfisher. Still, it had been a productive morning, as I had identified several suitable areas where kingfishers might breed. There had been no shortage of other wildlife to enhance the walk either: grey wagtails, dippers, a grey heron and a sparrowhawk were just some of the river's residents that had accompanied me. Much of the land I had explored that morning belonged to a friend of mine, so I decided to call in to him on the way back, since he had a great interest in the kingfisher.

As I made my way back through the undergrowth, the brambles became thicker and denser. Their tentacle-like stems snatched and snagged at my clothing, while their thorns bit into my hands and face. Eventually the wall of briars in front of me parted and I stepped, as though through a hidden gateway in the landscape, onto the manicured grass of my friend's lawn.

A driveway meandered through the greenness, climbing steeply upwards in a graceful, sweeping curve. Formal-looking cedar trees were dotted here and there, adding a touch of dignity and composure to the scene. As the lawns dropped away from the house, they melded into a wildwood of elder, ash and bramble: dignity became chaos, which in turn beheld beauty.

Coffee – properly brewed coffee – was the reward for this morning's efforts; that and companionship. As we sat in the kitchen talking about kingfishers, my eye was drawn to a glass case on the wall, in which sat a preserved kingfisher. Although the river was a couple of hundred metres below us, this kingfisher had flown up the hill and met its untimely demise by striking the glass of the conservatory on the side of the house. Possibly, it had been pursued by a sparrowhawk away from the river, and in its panic had not realized that the open space in front of it had been an illusion. Sadly, birds striking glass is a common occurrence, and many of them die from the head injuries they sustain on impact.

This bird had died decades ago but, thanks to the skill of the taxidermist, looked as fresh as though it had expired just the day before. The beauty of the bird and the richness of its colours inspired my friend to have the bird preserved. Even on that winter's morning, in the dull light of the kitchen, the colours on the kingfisher's plumage glowed with an otherworldly, almost ethereal light. Living close to a river, my friend had occasionally encountered kingfishers over the years, most while swimming. His encounters with the river and the kingfisher were forever immortalized by the poet John Mountfort when he penned 'The Kingfisher', describing my friend rather disingenuously as 'a blue-eyed monster'.

Our reverie over, and further inspired, I returned to the river and backtracked my way home. The angler had also departed; perhaps, like the Fisher King, once he had set me on the quest, he had returned to his own world. Like the angler, the Fisher King and the kingfisher itself, I required patience on this journey – a journey that was only beginning.

Patience is an attribute all naturalists must possess if they hope to study wildlife closely. Watching birds at their nests, and recording in intricate detail their behaviour, was nothing new for me. The kingfishers and great spotted woodpeckers were but the most recent in a long line of species that have piqued my interest since childhood. The attraction and fascination of watching the intimate family lives of birds is as hard to quantify as the enjoyment I derive from it. And not just to me, but also to my long-suffering parents, and unfortunate brothers and sister, who endured it throughout the early years of my upbringing.

Every bird that frequented our suburban garden was diligently recorded in a myriad of diaries, notebooks and loose scraps of paper, all of which I still have on my shelves today. If any of these visitors chose to nest, they were assured of five-star security and supervision. As long as it kept me occupied and didn't cause problems, my mother was happy to facilitate my obsession. She had long since given up trying to entice me into what others considered mainstream pursuits, such as sports or social activities. 'I think you prefer animals to people, don't you?' she enquired of me one day.

'Well,' I replied, 'they're easier to understand.'

Despite being an unpopular bird in many people's eyes, it was the magpie which claimed the trophy for being my first detailed nest study. In an adjoining garden, visible from my bedroom window, was a towering elm tree. Now long since felled, at the time it stood over fifteen metres tall. Dutch elm disease was prevalent during this period, and hedgerows across Ireland were dotted with the dead and decaying carcasses of these magnificent trees.

Dead for several years, the branches were bare and stark throughout the year. Skeletal boughs reached upward like outstretched arms, as though in a last, desperate plea for help, as the disease rampaged across the country, cutting down trees in the prime of their life. For several years, a pair of magpies had made their nest in the highest branches of my elm, clearly visible to my eager eyes and questioning mind. With no foliage to hide them, much of their family life was laid bare before me and dutifully written into my nest diary: 'Magpies – Vol. 1'.

Looking back on those diaries now, it seems incredible how much time I committed to this project, all the more so since I was young at the time – not even a teenager – and not overly renowned for my powers of concentration. From the time the birds started displaying, through nest-building, egg-laying and the rearing of their young, I carried out detailed and lengthy daily observations. On Saturdays and Sundays some of my observations spanned seven hours – in other words, a full working day for many adults! The single-minded, focused attention I applied to my interest did not bother me, but it certainly perplexed my family.

There was no time for me to help around the house, lay the table for Sunday dinner or tidy up afterwards – the birds might do something in my absence. My mother acquiesced, probably out of desperation for a quiet life, and let me spend hour after hour at the window on a sunny day staring skyward at a dead tree. However, she drew the line when I asked for my dinner to be served at my small window desk, insisting that the birds could wait while I joined the family at the table. Eating my dinner was always a hastily conducted affair on those days.

The magpie is unwelcome and unloved by many people due to its habit of preying on the nests of other birds. In the eyes of many it is a noisy, brash and cruel bird, and because of this it has been persecuted for many years. It is a survivor and adapts in conditions where other, less generalized species fail to thrive. Cats pose no threat to magpies, but our smaller garden birds have to cope both with natural predators, such as magpies, and introduced threats, such as cats. We humans often apply the strangest of 'rules' to nature, as though we were gods or somehow in control. For many, a lioness killing a day-old wildebeest is considered to be an exciting, dramatic event, worthy of being televised. Yet a magpie killing robin chicks is cruel and heartless.

During that spring of my pre-teen years those magpies became my friends, in a manner of speaking, and in a strange way, for a time, we grew up together. I watched the male, identifiable by his longer tail, proudly surveying his kingdom as the first morning rays set his plumage on fire in a blaze of iridescence. What had appeared as black radiated out in shades of purple, green and gold. He was dazzling. Sitting on the topmost branches, he would utter his distinctive rattling *chak-chak-chak-chak* call, each time accompanied by an upward flick of his long, glossy tail.

By comparison, I often sympathized with the female. Although both parents shared the duty of incubation, she seemed to take on most of the workload. Warm, sunny days, with her mate perched nearby, were undoubtedly pleasant as she sat exposed on the nest, incubating her eggs. But, with no foliage to shield her, the driving rain and sleet that fell on many other days showed no mercy, relentlessly pounding her.

I shared what I felt must have been their joy and elation as they reared their chicks from featherless, pink blobs to stubby-tailed caricatures of their parents many weeks later. My interpretations and inevitable personification of their behaviour were not scientific, nor were they ever supposed to be. I simply wrote down what I saw, for no other purpose than to record the world around me in a manner relevant to me. How many children of that age could apply themselves so single-handedly to a seemingly pointless task? Not many that I know of ... but then, I was never one of the many.

Despite my family's inability to share the natural world with me as eagerly as I might have hoped, they never shied away from defending it. A year or so later, I was coming home from a day out birdwatching by myself and had planned to meet my dad on his way home from the library. Every Saturday afternoon he walked there to change the books he'd borrowed the week before. I often met him afterwards and we would walk back home together. When I reached the agreed meeting point, he was already there with a friend, whom I had never met before. All fathers are proud of their sons, and mine was no exception. 'This is my youngest,' he exclaimed proudly.

There then began, for everyone, the tedious exploration of my achievements. Did I play football or rugby? No? Well, maybe tennis or hurling? A blank response greeted each enquiry, yet he persevered in the hope of finding common ground. But as well as not *playing* any sport, neither did I *watch* any – let alone 'follow' a team, a concept as alien today as it was back then.

My dad finally rescued the situation.

'He's not very good with people, he's happier with animals,' he said cheerfully. 'But he does know a lot about birds,' he added, followed by a thoughtful pause. 'And he knows *an awful* lot about magpies!'

# WATER UNDER THE BRIDGE

THE RIVER BELOW the bridge on which I stood was a broiling, seething mass of turbulence. The recent arrival of Storm Daniel had unleashed a quantity of water that I felt was more in keeping with Niagara Falls than a mountain stream in Ireland.

The power contained in the surging torrent below me was tremendous – gone was the quiet, bubbling and tranquil river that I knew from the summer months. In its place was a raging, out-of-control beast that had risen above its predetermined boundaries and engulfed habitat after habitat, home after home. The burrows of rabbits, wood mice, pygmy shrews and a host of other small creatures were now under half a metre of water that extended for over a hundred metres from the original banks. How had they fared? I wondered. Had there been enough time for them to escape, or had the rising waters been too quick and entombed them without warning? I despaired at the thought of their frightened, furry faces as the deluge inundated their refuges before carrying their lifeless bodies out with the current.

Looking at the racing and swirling monster below me was starting to make my head spin. Focusing intently on what your mind says should be unmoving can play havoc on your spatial awareness: with no warning, you can be sent careering down the proverbial rabbit hole on an increasingly chaotic journey involving a loss of perception. Or at least I find it so, and not always confined to moments such as these! I was coming back to earth, so to speak, when I heard an astounding outburst of birdsong coming from below me, despite the fact there was nowhere that I could see for a bird to sit.

Considering how early it was in the year, very little birdsong could be heard. Spring was rarely early in this part of Wicklow. The only birds singing in the past week had been robins and the occasional song thrush, the latter now sadly a declining species throughout Ireland due to habitat loss. It would be several months before the dawn chorus swelled to its oft-celebrated proportions with the participation of other thrushes, finches and a host of summer-visiting warblers.

And yet, that rich and cacophonous warbling continued to emanate from the torrent below. Frustrated, I scanned the parts of the banks that rose above the waters, but to no avail. I knew, from years of experience, what type bird it was; I just couldn't locate it. Finally, my eyes fell upon a rock protruding slightly from the eroded wall of a clay bank. Perched upon this small, rocky shelf was a dumpy, dark bird, about the size of a thrush. As I watched, it turned around to face me, revealing a startling white throat and upper breast – a dipper.

The dipper is a bird which many people in Ireland – to be fair, most people – do not even know exists. Yet it has held my fascination and respect since childhood, when I would cycle my Raleigh racing bike away from my suburban home in Blackrock to the nearby rivers and streams, which flowed through what, at that time, I thought of as the countryside.

Fast-flowing rivers, tumbling over rocks and carving their way through beds of shingle, are the home of this bird. Its entire life is often lived in a world the width of a river and along just a couple of kilometres of its length. The dipper is the sole member of its family in Ireland, with a further four species distributed throughout Asia and North and South America. It has a chunky body with a short tail, giving it a comical, rotund appearance. This is accentuated further by its habit of bobbing its body up and down every few seconds like a clockwork toy.

The plumage on the back, wings, tail and much of the underparts is blackish-brown, while the colour on its head is a slightly paler milk-chocolate brown. By stark contrast, the throat and breast are the purest white imaginable. Given that its habitat is usually a mixture of dark, reflective waters combined with swirling, white foam, I can only assume its colouration is a form of camouflage.

The plumage of both sexes is identical, which makes telling them apart a tricky business. When seen together, the male is noticeably larger than the female. However, it is hard to gauge size when birds are seen alone or flying past. Close study of a pair standing together often identifies individual differences between them. Compared to the female, the male usually has a slightly broader band of mahogany-red between the white breast and sooty-black underparts. With practice, this small detail can be readily used in combination with 'a feel' for the size of the bird to suggest whether a lone bird is male or female. I was very fortunate with the pair that I was watching in that the female was quite noticeably smaller. Furthermore, she had an unusual mark on her underparts where the white bled into the reddish-brown band, creating a readily identifiable 'tattoo'.

The dipper is a member of the Passerine group of birds, commonly known as perching birds. However, it is unique amongst these in that it can both dive and swim. If it is not seen sitting on a stone in the river, it is usually found foraging about in the river itself, often with only its head and shoulders visible above the surface. It has several adaptions to this peculiar lifestyle, which enable it to live in such a challenging environment.

Being a perching bird, it does not have webbed feet, but its strong claws and legs provide excellent grip on the stony riverbed as it battles against the strong currents, which continuously buffet it while it's trying to feed. In deeper water, it uses its short and rounded wings to 'fly' underwater against the flow of the river. This enables it to stay in the same spot as it probes under stones with its short beak, searching for mayfly and caddisfly larvae, upon which it feeds.

Spending so much time both in and under the water, the bird's feathers need to be waterproof, otherwise it would quickly chill and die. It always fascinates me how water droplets roll off their backs, like silver beads of mercury rolling around on a tabletop, each one splitting into smaller and smaller globules before falling onto the stones below and breaking into a myriad of tiny droplets like shattered glass.

Perhaps the most surprising thing about this bird, for me, is its song. It is rich, loud and melodic, not unlike that of a blackbird. The clarity and loudness of the notes are always surprising as they soar above the crashing sounds of the river, clearly audible for some distance. One of the main reasons that birds sing is to proclaim ownership of a territory, this being the area in which they will live and rear their family. As such, most birds only sing in the spring, when the nesting season commences. The dipper is unusual in that it can be heard singing throughout most of the year. It does so because it continually maintains and defends its territory along a chosen stretch of river.

Although they are usually portrayed as a characteristic species of fast-flowing rivers, in some parts of Ireland, dippers can be found at sea level. My enthusiasm for this species was forged at an early age, despite living in a housing estate in Blackrock – a considerable distance from any montane torrents or glaciated river valleys.

When I was a young teenager, my Raleigh bike, complete with down-swept racing handlebars, was my trusted friend and companion, enabling me to explore the periphery of the built-up world in which I lived. While far from what people describe as countryside, this periphery was less built-up than where I lived. Open areas of wasteland and fields bordered onto houses with large gardens, which themselves would then graduate into the ranks of houses that made up the suburban housing estates. At every opportunity I would head off alone to explore the natural wonders around me, and nothing attracted me more than a river.

What was it about them that held my interest? There were parks with small areas of woodland and a variety of beaches and shorelines to explore, yet rivers pulled at me, reeling me in like a fish on a line. Was it that memory of the kingfisher I saw with my father? Several years had passed since that encounter and I had yet to come across another, despite endless searching. No, it wasn't the kingfisher that drew me – it was the river itself.

There is something magical, no matter what age you are, about lying on your chest on a grassy bank, staring at the water below, surrounded by the intoxicating scents of midsummer waterside herbage: water mint, elder, watercress, iris and countless others. The soothing, tinkling and bubbling sounds of the river made the world around me quiet – it was possible to immerse myself into this riparian universe and escape the noise, the senseless chaos that the rest of the world presented to me. That river I cycled to was only a few miles from my home, and I regularly travelled there by myself from the age of twelve or thirteen.

However, I was not alone, although I may have appeared so to others: a pair of dippers had made this river their home. I used to spend hours just lying there, watching them flying past me, up and down the river. Like feathered projectiles, they sped to and from the nest that they had made deep under a culvert buried beneath a nearby dual carriageway. Having been shown the river by my father on one of our Sunday forays, I often returned to catch sticklebacks or just to explore. The initial sighting of one of the dippers sent me running for my bird book. This was my first encounter with this species, and their uniqueness and differences from other, more familiar, species enthralled me.

On my excited return at the end of the day, I tried explaining their fascinating abilities and lifestyles to my family over dinner. As they shook their heads, either in wonder or despair, it was hard to tell if this was directed at the birds or at me. It was not just the dippers that drew me to that flowing paradise; there were endless treasures and discoveries to keep my young mind occupied.

Sticklebacks darted around in the shallow water, and the bright red and green colours of the male proved irresistible to my inquisitive mind. Stalking them with the same stealth and zeal of a heron, I nimbly and expertly scooped them up in my makeshift shrimp net. Safely secured in jam jars, they bounced around in my knapsack as I cycled my way home, where I carefully transferred them to one of the many aquariums in my bedroom.

These were not the only aquatic wonders I brought back. I transported and decanted great diving beetles and their ferocious-looking larvae, which resembled some nightmarish creation from the darkest recesses of the mind. As well as water beetles, I discovered dragonfly larvae, caddisfly larvae, ramshorn snails, pond skaters and many more. I kept them in aquariums, in basins, in jars – in fact, in anything that could hold water. I kept a wide range of water-loving fauna, along with other creatures from a variety of habitats, throughout the house, conservatory and garden. I kept them to study, to learn from and sometimes simply just to watch. In some ways, growing up, they were my friends, and as such I shared my bedroom with them.

The layout of my bedroom was modelled, to the best of my father's ability, on a plan for a naturalist's study adapted from Gerald Durrell's book *The Amateur Naturalist*. Part library, part zoo and part museum, it was an amalgam of function, necessity and artistic display. Academic aspects of the natural world rubbed shoulders with living specimens, which in turn stood alongside preserved specimens, all collected and labelled with care.

My extensive library of nature books and wildlife magazines ranged from pristine and barely used to well-worn and held together with Sellotape: in hindsight, I must have been a very easy child to buy Christmas and birthday presents for. The bookshelves, carefully designed by my dad, provided extensive display space for a range of natural curios I acquired: a bizarre blend of rocks, fossils, seashells and birds' feathers. Pride of place at the time, however, went to a small, stuffed crocodile.

Many years before I was born, an uncle of mine had travelled to Cairo, and on his return he presented my parents with a gift of a preserved baby Nile crocodile. For many years as I grew up it graced our living room, gradually becoming more battered by my extensive handling. The tip of its tail had long since broken off, exposing the wire frame inside, as well as the horsehair stuffing.

My dad somehow Sellotaped the damaged tail back on, several times, but each repair was less successful than the last. Eventually my mother decided that a dead reptile held together with yellowing, nicotine-stained plastic no longer suited her décor, and it was demoted to the rubbish bin. But a specimen as precious this, in my eyes, could not be consigned to the bin, and it spent many years on my bedroom shelf as a prized natural-history specimen.

Squashed between the various makeshift aquariums were numerous large sweet jars with holes cut into their lids for ventilation. These were filled with grasses, twigs and leaves, and were home to a range of caterpillars, ladybirds, grasshoppers, butterflies and other insects. The warm, intoxicating scent that arose from these jars on hot days was a pungent blend of fermenting grass juice and ladybird poo.

While not fetid, it was certainly aromatic, and, from my mother's perspective, not in a healthy way. During the late spring and early summer months, when my collection became most extensive, the containers were moved outside to the greenhouse. There, for the most part, they happily thrived amongst my father's rows of carefully nurtured seedlings. Coincidently, many of the aquatic insect larvae that I kept and reared in my bedroom aquariums, such as caddisfly and mayfly larvae, were also the favoured food of dippers.

I would usually encounter the dippers each time I returned to the river. At the time, I never went there exclusively to watch them; they were simply part of the waterside habitat I explored. Sometimes I lay on my chest in the riverbank herbage and watched them for hours. Other days I spent considerably less, dedicating my time instead to collecting numerous natural-history specimens to bring back home. And now, years later, I was once again watching dippers.

ALTHOUGH I HAD been observing dippers from the early years of my youth, this in no way took away from the enjoyment and happiness I now felt as I watched the bird singing from the rock below the bridge where I stood. And although I intended to search the valleys through which this river flowed in search of kingfishers in the coming months, I knew there was plenty of time to explore and watch other wonders.

The kingfisher is a late breeder, and for obvious reasons. The raging floodwaters beneath me were unpredictable; in a few days they would likely subside, and the open-faced mudbanks would once again be exposed alongside the water. However, given the time of year, further inundations in the coming weeks and months were not only likely, they were virtually inevitable.

The kingfisher's nesting burrow is dug into these mudbanks, often only a short distance above the surface of the river. The unpredictable rising and falling of water levels in the early spring make it a risky business excavating a burrow, which could be flooded with no warning. By the time late April has arrived, the river will be less likely to flood, and this is when the kingfishers will commence the business of raising a family. April was several months away yet, and there would be few opportunities to watch kingfishers along the river before then.

The dippers, however, had no concerns about the unpredictable nature of the weather; they are an early-breeding species. Although nest-building in the Wicklow Mountains does not occur until February, at the very earliest, there is usually plenty of preparatory breeding activity by early January. What better birds to study than the kingfisher's neighbours, while awaiting the return of the Fisher King himself?

It was cold and only about an hour after sunrise. Because the river was in the lee of a hill, it would be another few hours before the sun's rays would light up the stones at the water's edge. The air was crisp; not surprisingly, since the temperature during the previous night had dipped below minus five degrees Celsius. The water levels of the river had returned to a more normal depth for this time of year, and a small amount of clay bank was exposed. The grass on the top of this bank was covered in white frost, and small needles of ice extended from the tips, arching out over the water. Ice covered wherever the water was still enough to allow the crystals to form. Sharply pointed daggers of wafer-thin ice extended from the bank in a series of isosceles triangles, turning the bank into the mouth of a fearsome beast filled with teeth.

Despite the cold weather, the dippers were in a mind for breeding. All through the winter they had remained along the river, coping with the changing water levels with the tenacity of a limpet. I rarely saw them together, and they could be found anywhere along the kilometre stretch of river that was their home. Sometimes I just heard their call, a metallic-sounding *zink*, as one zipped past me low over the water. Other times I saw one feeding wherever the water was shallow enough to allow it.

But now, with the start of the breeding season approaching, they began to spend more time together. Unlike in previous months, they could now often be found foraging along the edge of the river within proximity of each other. Furthermore, instead of ranging over the entire length of their territory, they began regularly to frequent the water around a large bridge that crossed the river.

Dippers build a dome-shaped, enclosed nest with a small entrance hole. Although they often use a natural nesting site, such as amongst twisted tree roots protruding from the eroded banks of the river, many prefer man-made structures like bridges or culverts. Built high up against the stone buttresses, they can withstand all but the worst storm waters. These structures, especially if they are built from stone, often have ledges or protruding stones – perfect for placing a nest out of harm's way. Being located above water and with no access from above or below, they are extremely unlikely to be attacked by predators. Once a nest site has been chosen, it is often used by successive generations of dippers. Some sites I know of have had dippers nesting under the same bridge arch for several decades.

However, although they may use the same nest site in successive years, the nest itself is usually rebuilt, or at the very least repaired each year, since it rarely survives completely intact for the ten months after the young birds leave. The nest is constructed from a variety of mosses, both aquatic and terrestrial, and lined with grasses and leaves. Sadly, as humans affect the environment more and more, nests have now been discovered incorporating non-natural materials: polypropylene twine, polyurethane, plastic and even fishing line, all used under the mistaken illusion they are grasses. What effect this has on the birds and the environment itself is not known, but it is unlikely to be beneficial.

When first developed, plastic must have seemed like a wonderful invention, and indeed it is – but we are now drowning in our creation. The more we study the problem, the more we realize that we are responsible for killing so many living creatures through our lack of foresight, our lack of understanding and, at a basic level, our lack of compassion for other forms of life.

Garden birds such as robins and blackbirds now build their nests using plastic; seabirds feed plastic in error to their young; and the sea itself is becoming a soup of plastic beads, so dense in parts that it poses a real threat to life. The more I looked around the river with its flotsam of bobbing, multicoloured plastics, the more I despaired.

Like the great spotted woodpeckers in the nearby woods, dippers often use their nests to roost in during the winter months. The woodpecker returns to the nesting tree in the last moments of daylight, flying across the fields and woods over which it has roved during the day. In the same manner, the dipper returns to the same bridge where its nest was located, working its way back along the foaming water and shiny, weed-covered rocks where it spent its day foraging. If the nest has been washed away by early winter storms, the dipper will continue to return. But, with no nest to roost in, it will pass the hours of darkness sleeping on the actual ledge where the nest once stood.

The tumultuous and chaotic scene below the bridge posed an immediate problem. I needed to go under it to inspect the nest site, since I had no idea whether last year's nest still survived or not. During the summer months, when water levels were lower, I had often walked along a ledge that ran alongside the base of each arch. Even then, this ledge was below water, but only by about fifteen or twenty centimetres.

Undoubtedly it was now considerably deeper, and the ledge was likely to be a metre or more under water, which, combined with a fast-flowing current, made the idea of going under quite daunting. Wearing a pair of chest-high fisherman's waders, I slipped and slithered my way down the bank and into the water.

Looking at the dark, uninviting depths ahead of me, I was glad I had opted for a lifejacket over my coat; I had no wish to become a river-fatality statistic. The force of the water pressing against my legs was incredible as I pushed myself along against the current. Using my hands and gripping handfuls of the scant vegetation on the bank, I gradually pulled, pushed and willed myself closer to the arch until I was able to examine the bridge walls.

A smooth, concrete finish extended upwards from one side of the river and across the expansive vault, before merging back into the flowing water on the other side. Several protruding rocks formed a broken line about a metre above the swirling current; it was on one of these rocks that the dippers had successfully raised a family last year. But of that nest not a trace now remained. The rock on which that masterfully knitted creation had sat was as bare and stark as the grey concrete that covered the wall alongside.

I was both surprised and disappointed by this discovery. The water level of the river had not risen that high in the previous months, so it certainly hadn't been washed away. Something else must have happened … I wondered what. If a predator had disturbed the nest in the past few months while birds were roosting there, then it was unlikely they would choose to nest there this season after all.

The bright, crisp days of the early new year did not last long. The calendar may have stated it was January – effectively still the middle of winter – yet it felt like spring. Daytime temperatures had recently hit twelve degrees Celsius, and when the sun shone the air felt balmy. This had a predictable effect on the local birds: rather than focusing on simply finding food and day-to-day survival, their minds turned to breeding and to love.

The rich, soprano fluting notes of song thrushes erupted from the trees, and blue tits began performing their butterfly display flights. These were a joy to watch and banished all feelings of the winter blues. The male blue tit would perch in the sunshine at the top of a bush, singing his delicate, high-pitched, trilling song while a female watched below. Then he would launch himself into the air and glide past her on outspread wings and fanned tail. While gliding, he would gently flutter his wings, making himself look like a giant, blue-and-yellow butterfly.

The dippers were not immune to this onset of romance, and the river resonated with the vibrant tones of their songs as the birds began their courtship for the coming season. The song of the dipper is certainly one of my favourites, yet it is a song with which so many people are unfamiliar or may not even notice. In many ways it is like a mixture of three of Ireland's best songsters – the song thrush, the blackbird and the blackcap, a small, summer-visiting warbler from southern Europe and North Africa. The dipper has the fast warbling qualities of the blackcap's song, the flute-like tones of the blackbird's and the high-pitched clarity of the song thrush's.

The song is loud because it needs to be heard over the sound of the river. Unlike most other Irish birds, both the male and female sing, but predominantly it is the male who performs. Usually the song is delivered from a rock in the middle of the river; ironically, this is often where the noise of the churning water is at its loudest. It is surprisingly far-reaching, and can often be heard from a hundred metres or so away.

The late-winter courtship of dippers can be a complex affair, and sometimes it can be hard to interpret. I would spend hours sitting on the riverbank watching them, yet I became so engrossed in their performances that often it felt as though only a short period of time had passed. Both the male and female dipper defend separate territories along the river – the male's territory often including the previous season's nest site. I knew from earlier observations that during the autumn and early winter the male would often chase the female away if she strayed into his territory. Now his late-winter singing informs the female that it is safe to approach him – and when she does, landing beside him on a stone, a theatrical performance like no other begins.

Standing on a wet and moss-covered rock in the middle of the surging river, the male stretches his body as tall as possible and points his bill straight up in the air. He then spreads his wings and flutters them rapidly while fanning his tail. Looking not unlike a ballet dancer performing an allegro, he dances around the female, singing loudly all the time. Meanwhile, the female watches, crouching down on the rock in front of him, seemingly in awe of his dancing prowess. Then, prompted by an unseen signal, she stands up and points her bill skyward in a similar manner, and both birds begin to touch each other's bills. This is often referred to as bill-fencing, and the two birds begin to joust like comical swordfighters.

ONE MORNING IN January 2018, while I was watching a duelling pair of dippers, a third bird unexpectedly arrived on an adjacent rock and began to flutter his outspread wings, singing loudly as he did so – an intruding male. Furious at this interloper, the resident male turned away from his prospective mate and began challenging his rival.

The noise of the river was temporarily muted by the loudness of their challenging songs, and while the two males were engrossed in their threatening vocalizations, the female flew away downstream. The resident male then made a lunge at the intruder, forcing him off the rock and to retreat upstream in defeat, pursued by the triumphant resident male. Their harsh and aggressive *zit-zit-zit* calls as they flew away were in marked contrast to the melodic-sounding performance I had enjoyed earlier.

The dippers continued to sing, dance and joust over the following weeks, but of the kingfishers there was no sign. It was as though they had simply melted away into the unknown, and it would be some time before I encountered them again. With each passing week the dippers performed their duets with more and more enthusiasm. And, despite my vigilance, I witnessed no further sorties into their territory by challenging rivals.

The male's valiant efforts and dancing prowess finally yielded results in late January when the female, solicited by his singing, crouched on a rock in front him. Spreading her wings out, she embraced the wet surface of the stone while he mated with her, surrounded by the tumultuous roar of the river that was their home. With the defence of their territory established, and a successful sealing of their union, everything was set for breeding season. I was hopeful they would choose their nest site in the coming weeks and actively start building by early February. Many dippers lay their eggs by late February, and I expected these to be no different.

But by early February the weather had changed. The daytime temperatures had gradually been decreasing, following the formation of a polar vortex over northern Europe. This dramatic weather pattern was not confined to plummeting thermal readings; it unleashed an assault of snow from the continent, the like of which had not been seen here for almost ten years; the snowfall was fast, furious and heavy. Accumulations were such that in the space of two hours the main roads in the area were hidden by a whiteout, and within twelve hours were impassable. They would remain so for several days.

While the Lapland-like landscape brought a welcome escape from daily routines for children (and some adults), for much of our wildlife it brought hunger and hardship. The fast-flowing river was in no danger of freezing over, but the banks disappeared under piles of snow. Ice extended into the river as far as possible before the swift current eroded it away. The shingle beds and rocks essential to the dippers' survival simply disappeared under quantities of snow.

When faced with adverse weather, birds often perform what is referred to as 'altitudinal migration'. This is when a species that is usually non-migratory carries out a local movement to a lower altitude in order to avoid inclement conditions. The birds then return when favourable conditions resume. Kingfishers would be one of the first river birds to respond to this onslaught of snow, and I knew there was little if any chance of these birds remaining in the area. The frozen water close to the bank would prevent them from feeding, and the dangers of diving deeply into half-frozen, ice-cold water were clear.

Following rivers downstream for many kilometres, the kingfishers would arrive at the coast and the rich estuarine feeding grounds, where the river merges with the sea. There, they would feed predominantly on prawns and the fry of various fish species. They make a colourful sight when seen against a backdrop of the dark-grey mud and steel-coloured water. A cold winter's day birdwatching on the Irish coast is always enhanced by a glimpse of this jewel of the river.

By comparison, dippers are arguably less fortunate. Deep coastal waters may provide excellent fishing opportunities, but they are of no help to a bird that feeds in shallow water. Dippers must endure the inclement conditions as much as possible, feeding on the surface of the rocks or probing deep under the banks amongst any vegetation that may have escaped the worst of the snow. Other insect-eating birds, such as the wren, suffer terribly, and up to 90 per cent of a local population can be killed during a severe cold snap such as this.

My dippers stayed in their territory for as long as possible. I saw them during the first few days of those Arctic-like conditions. Hunched up and sitting on the snow-covered rocks, they both looked miserable. Rarely did I see them feeding, and after a few days they too were gone, along with the resident grey wagtails. They would probably have had to travel many miles downstream before finding conditions suitable to sustain them. It was impossible to follow them due to the impassable minor roads, and I was unable to ascertain where they had fled to.

The dangers these birds faced from cold weather became all too real for me as I walked along the banks in search of them. It was impossible to know the location of the bank's edge, and a smooth, unbroken blanket of white gently curved from the surrounding woods into the water. There was no definition of form or contour. Gently feeling the ground beneath me with each step, I carefully progressed along the river's edge. Suddenly there was no ground below me and I was in sub-zero-temperature water almost up to my waist!

It is hard to convey the shock of such freezing water pouring into my wellingtons and soaking through the cloth of my jeans to well above knee height. My breath was sucked out of my body in an instant, and the first inhalation was met with burning pain throughout my lower extremities. I struggled through the water trying to find a way out, and eventually found an overhanging branch. I pulled myself out of the water and collapsed into a heap of snow. I desperately pulled off my wellingtons, pouring out a couple of litres of water from each boot in the process. This hardly raised my spirits, as already I had no feeling whatsoever in my feet. I was some distance from home with no change of clothes – was frostbite a possibility, I wondered?

Putting my feet back into the boots, I started to make my way homewards, but my numbed feet were unwilling to respond to my body's commands. Navigating my way, as though in a drunken stupor, through deep snow, with no feeling from a little below the waist, was an experience I hope never to repeat. Finally reaching my destination, I bathed my frozen, putty-coloured limbs in a warm bath and endured the 'welcome' pain of returning circulation. It was a lesson not to be forgotten.

The experience of such water heightened my admiration for all the birds that had to endure these challenging conditions: kingfishers, dippers, goosanders and grey wagtails to name but a few. It is easy to assume that, because these birds have some degree of waterproofing, the water poses few problems. However, kingfishers in Amsterdam and Bavaria have been found completely frozen in a diving position, either in ice or in the water just below the ice.

It is unlikely that they died immediately on entering the water. Possibly the shock of the cold water weakened them so that they lacked the energy to fly out of the water before their feathers became saturated. Another possibility is that after diving in they rose to the surface, became trapped under the ice and drowned. Either way, these poor, unfortunate individuals clearly show the risks involved in finding food in extreme weather.

The German word for kingfisher is *Eisvogel*, which literally means 'ice bird'. It may refer to birds such as those mentioned previously, found frozen in the ice. Another thought is that the blue colouration on its plumage is likened to ice blue. Either way, snow and ice are something that drives kingfishers away, and I did not expect the *Eisvogel* to return until the approach of the breeding season, many weeks hence.

But the snow and ice, despite all its ferocity, did not survive the gradually lengthening hours of sunlight, and after a week it had sufficiently cleared for me to easily navigate the river system once more. The dippers and grey wagtails had returned before the last of the snow had melted, but as yet they had no interest in any further breeding behaviour. I was glad to be able to return to my riverbank wanderings, and the dippers provided enough motivation for my daily observations as I awaited the return of the kingfishers from their coastal wintering quarters.

The late-winter sun was still an hour or so above the horizon. Already the air was rapidly cooling, with the promise of a frosty night to come. The clouds had started to show the firework display of colours that signalled the day's end as I walked along the river. Steam fog, formed by water vapour rising from the river and meeting the fast-cooling air above, drifted upwards in swirling tendrils, coils and wisps. They looked like a living entity reaching from the river towards the sky. Patches of snow lingered on the banks and on the track alongside the river. Anywhere the sun had failed to reach was still in the grip of the Arctic blast.

As I approached a small, weir-like formation, consisting of a line of rocks that crossed the river, I heard a loud, clear whistle: *peeeeee-peeeeee*. I turned around, looking for the kingfisher, since I was sure that was what was calling, but there was no sign of any flying past. Again, I heard the call, *peeeeee*. I scanned the river with my binoculars but found nothing. It was a familiar-sounding whistle, yet it did not sound completely right for a kingfisher. What other bird whistled as clearly? None that I could think of.

Moments passed and another *peeeeee* sounded in the clear air, almost in front of me. I scanned the far bank and a ripple in the water in the middle of the river brought clarity to the situation: it was no bird that called; it was a mammal, an otter. No sooner had I realized my mistake than a whiskered face popped up out of the water and quickly submerged with a flick of its long, tapering tail in the air. Its appearance brought a crescendo of noise from the bankside opposite me: *peeeeee-peeeeee ... peeeeee ...* Not just one otter, I now realized, but a family of them.

The mother continued diving and then surfacing in the pool formed upstream by the weir. She was actively hunting for her pups, hidden under the overhanging bank. I watched, unnoticed, behind a holly bush, and over the next half-hour saw the two pups swim out from their hiding place and follow their mother around the pool in search of fish. Two pups, sometimes called kittens, is a normal-sized litter for otters in Ireland, and they can be born at any time of the year. These pups were half-grown and would likely spend much of the coming year with her.

Sometimes the youngsters stayed hidden below the grassy overhangs, their faces just visible in the gloomy shadows. Other times they swam in tandem with their mother, the three of them in a line as though she was towing them along – and perhaps they were holding on to her, it was hard to be sure. All the time I watched them, they were unaware of my presence, as though I were a ghost in the landscape, there but not there.

They swam, ducked, dived and played, quite simply enjoying life. As the mist rose around them, shrouding them in white streamers, they rolled around together in the water, tumbling, squirming and whistling. Moments like this are rare, for animals and humans alike, and I knew I was watching something very special: that private point in time between a parent and their children, that close moment when time seems to stop and the world around ceases to exist ...

The otters' unawareness of me made me feel like an intruder, and I was almost relieved when dusk began to encroach and the trio of water-lovers swam further upstream, melting into the snow-laden landscape. And with them, with that magical moment set in a fantasy land, travelled the Arctic beast. The following day brought rain, and the remaining white landscape disappeared over the coming days as though it had never been – the otters also disappeared, and I never saw the family again.

With a rise in temperatures, the dippers wasted no time in resuming their breeding programme, and within a few days I saw the female on a rock, which was covered with a layer of moss, glistening green as the water flowed over it. She was tugging at it – a large piece came free and, holding it tightly in her bill, she flew upstream, disappearing from view. I was fairly sure I knew where she was going, and as I made my way after her a small, stone bridge came into view. Only wide enough for a single car, it was a quiet and relatively undisturbed piece of stonework.

As I approached the bridge, a dipper flew out from underneath the roof: *zit-zit*, it called as it shot past me. Although dippers will often use natural nest sites such as tree roots or underneath an overhanging rock, they will almost always use a bridge if a suitable one occurs within their territory. Modern road bridges are often unsuitable, as there are no ledges or protruding stones upon which to build a nest. This small bridge was different in its design, and a pipe underneath, located about one-third of the way from the other side, provided a suitable ledge on which to build.

Both male and female are involved in nest-building, and although the pair had only started in the past few days, the nest was well under way and taking shape. The foundation was of waterweed, moss and other aquatic plants, and this was what the pair were building at the moment. As they worked together over the following days and weeks, the nest eventually grew into the familiar, dome-shaped structure. The exterior was a thick layer of green moss, which darkened with age until it became almost black. Inside was a completely different construction: a tightly woven cup of strong, pliable plant roots and grasses, lined with soft grass.

These two different aspects of the nest were usually constructed separately, with the fixed, woven cup being built upon the mossy base and then the domed walls built up around it. It can take up to three weeks for dippers to build this masterpiece, but this pair managed it within a two-week period. When it was finished, there was a small, circular entrance hole in the wall of the nest facing the water, angled slightly downwards.

The nest was located directly above the deepest part of the river. Although there was a shallow ledge running under the bridge, allowing me to see the nest, it was impossible to get up close to it. A deep pool, several metres in depth and formed through erosion, lay under the bridge, two-thirds of the way across. It intrigued me as to how they could have known this, or even if they did. A nest positioned above permanent water is far safer than one built in a location that may become accessible to predators due to changing water levels.

At this time of year, when the river was still high with meltwater and run-off from rain, the river extended from bank to bank and was of reasonable depth. However, in several months' time a shore would extend from the banks towards a narrow, deep channel in the centre. How the dippers could have known this and built accordingly was nothing short of incredible. It suggested an understanding and an ability above my own – a slightly unnerving thought, to say the least.

Once the nest is completed, there is generally a delay of a week or two before the eggs are laid. Naturally, the egg-laying date is dependent on the nest being finished. However, a two- to three-week construction schedule is often delayed, or brought forward, depending on weather and resultant water levels. Often the only way to know whether the eggs have been laid is when, through long observation, the female is noted to be incubating or appears far less often along the river's edge.

By early March, the nest had been completed for over a week, yet there were no indications of egg-laying. Both the male and female were still seen sitting together on the rocks downstream from the nest for extended periods. Content in each other's company, they often sat in the sun, their half-closed, white eyelids catching the sun. Their mahogany breast-bands, fading to chestnut, glowed with a rich lustre, in strong contrast with their pristine, white bellies.

The white eyelids that I could see on the birds in front of me are not unique to dippers. However, because dippers seem to blink a lot, their eyelids appear prominently against their dark-plumaged heads. Even at considerable distances it is possible, through binoculars, to see the flash of white each time a bird blinks its eyes. The purpose of this colouration is not yet known, but it has been proposed that the birds may use it as a signalling mechanism, as they live in a habitat where they can struggle to be heard against the background noise of the river.

As I watched the pair early one morning, I heard a loud whistle from behind me, a whistle that cut through the air and all other surrounding sounds. Before I could turn around to locate it, a bullet of intense and vivid blue sped past me, calling loudly, *peeeeee ... peeeeee ... peeeeee ...*

The kingfisher's plumage gleamed in the morning sunlight. The wings and head were a dark royal blue, speckled with flecks of black and white, creating an intricate chequerboard effect. Against this deep blue, the vibrant, azure tail and rump truly glowed in contrast: it almost pulsed, so startling was its iridescence. Turning its body slightly sideways as it banked around a bend in the river, the blaze of blue was replaced by an orange that mellowed the image on my eyes and made it more acceptable and less startling. In the briefest of moments, it had flashed past and was gone.

Just the echo of its passing lingered.

# THE QUEST

THAT UNEXPECTED BOLT of blue, that speeding blue bullet, was a kingfisher – and it had an unexpected effect on me. It grounded me.

Of course, the fact that I had actually seen one was not a surprise in itself, as I had glimpsed them regularly throughout past years along this river. What *was* a surprise was that I realized I had almost forgotten about them, having become increasingly captivated by the antics of my family of dippers. But the whistling cry that hung in the air, reverberating off the low-arched stone bridge through which the kingfisher had flown, signalled its return and the beginning of my search. The sighting of that kingfisher confirmed that the snow was well and truly banished and that spring was returning. Only when conditions have begun to become more favourable will they return for anything other than a passing visit. And when they do, their arrival to stay is often heralded by its stirring cry, as was the case just then.

Kingfishers are often reported in literature as being both early breeders and a species that can have between two and three broods in a year. Many of these reports refer to birds in England or birds living on lowland rivers. There, it is not unusual for kingfishers to be actively displaying in courtship and mating by late February or early March. But the birds on my river did not fall into this category. Hugely variable temperatures, unpredictable rainfall and rapidly changing river levels are all features which can make the Wicklow Mountains a challenging place to make a riverside home.

Rivers are like people. They have different life stages, unpredictable moods and erratic personalities. Some kingfishers made their homes in rivers that were in the final stages of their journeys, approaching the sea, slow-flowing and meandering, with banks built up by years of deposition and erosion. But the rivers that flow through the Wicklow Mountains are in the youthful stage of life. Free, untamed, with endless and uncontained energy, they bound down the mountainsides like hyperactive children. Through the primal forces of erosion over eons of time, they carve out rivulets, then channels, then gorges and eventually valleys. Rocks, born of fire millennia ago, ripped open by monstrous glaciers several kilometres high, have since been carved and shaped, their contours softened by the rivers' flowing power.

Due to the topography of the Wicklow Mountains, much of this river had banks made of rock and stone, as well as shallow, rapidly flowing water that chattered its way along rock-laden riverbeds. All of this meant that considerable stretches of the river were unsuitable for kingfishers, through no fault of the river itself. Kingfishers were simply not designed for this type of habitat. However, nature, if nothing else, is wonderfully adaptive, and an enterprising species can forge an existence in the most challenging of circumstances.

The valleys this river flowed through had been carved out initially by glaciers, then further eroded by the river itself. Glacial deposits of boulder clay were deposited at irregular intervals, which then provided the opportunity for broadleaved trees such as mountain ash, oak and silver birch to colonize.

Millennia of accumulating leaf litter now provided a further thin layer of soil over the underlying bedrock. The river's erosive action easily shaped the boulder clay, whenever it encountered any, into banks that in theory were suitable for kingfishers to nest in. And so, in the Wicklow Mountains, they had become a species associated with woodland and rivers rather than just open-river habitat.

Unlike dippers, kingfishers are distributed thinly along this river, and their territories are large and, for the most part, discontinuous. The population density of breeding dippers was effectively at its maximum along this stretch of water. This was easy enough to see while walking along the riverbank, watching a dipper flying ahead of me. When it reached the end of its territory, it simply turned around and flew past me the way I had come. If I walked past this point, I would usually encounter another dipper within a very short distance – a different territory. So suited was this river to their requirements that, almost without exception, each dipper territory bordered another for many kilometres in an unbroken chain. This was not the case with kingfishers.

Their territories were larger but were impossible to measure as accurately as those of the dippers, since, rather than conveniently flying short distances ahead of me, the kingfishers I saw simply disappeared around the furthest corner of the river with the acceleration of a bullet. Their territory had to encompass both a suitable breeding site and several productive feeding sites. Whereas in the dippers' world these two requirements often happily coexist – and I have regularly seen dippers feeding only a few metres from their nest – the kingfishers' requirements involved a lot more wing-power.

Two good feeding areas could easily be separated by a couple of hundred metres of unsuitable shallow and fast-flowing water. Furthermore, any exposed bank suitable for breeding could be located several hundred metres from the nearest fishing pool. This did not mean that unsuitable stretches of river could not be part of the kingfishers' territory – they formed the conduits which joined the various elements of their lifestyle together.

With many other species, it was possible to identify a general area of suitable habitat as the key requirement for locating a territory. Locating kingfisher territories along this river would mean identifying key locations, both for feeding and nesting, then hopefully joining the dots to make a picture. This was going to involve a lot of walking, a lot of waiting and a lot of luck. I did not mind the long treks and neither did my dog. She absolutely loved the fact that I had to do so much walking, as it meant she got to accompany me to all sorts of interesting places.

My plans for any given day dictated how much time she spent with me. If I was exploring the countryside, navigating my way along rivers and through woodlands, then she was allowed to accompany me throughout. However, if I needed to sit quietly for an hour or two, hidden on the riverbank, then she had to wait in the car for my return – she strongly disliked those days! Occasionally, if I was sitting in a hide for a whole day watching woodpeckers, or it was simply too hot to leave her in the car, she had to stay at home and await my return. She absolutely hated those days, and her sorrowful eyes and softly wagging tail on my departure did nothing to encourage me. But today, and the weeks ahead, were times of companionship and combined trailblazing – a season of happiness for us both.

NOW THAT THE kingfishers had returned, I started to enjoy more regular sightings. Though I saw the dippers every day without exception, the kingfishers were not as quick to give up their secrets. Some days I saw them only once, other days several times – and many days not at all. But with each passing week, I became more acquainted with both their lives and the world they lived in.

I stared at the bare branches of the willow tree ahead of me. It was not noteworthy for any particular reason, other than that it was there. Its spindly branches reached out across the water and the furthest leaves intermittently dipped in and out of the water, like a person tentatively checking the water temperature. I was reminded of summer days, when I was a teenager and languishing in a boat, trailing my fingers in the water and watching similar patterns form and disappear – the void separating the years was traversed by the river.

I refocused my attention on the tree in front of me. I was at least twenty metres away, but all I saw was a tree. On several previous occasions, as I had passed the same tree, a kingfisher had unexpectedly flown out and disappeared before I had a chance even to raise my binoculars. The first couple of times, it had flown downstream along a well-wooded and heavily overgrown stretch of river, effectively disappearing into a tangled wall of branches after a very short distance. It was impossible to know how far it had flown after this point, and past searches had never produced a second sighting.

More recently it had flown directly across the river and disappeared into the dense oakwood opposite me. I had never encountered this behaviour before, and it puzzled me immensely. Although many other kingfisher species in different parts of the world lived in woodland, this species did not. The kingfishers I had watched on other rivers behaved in a more typical fashion; when disturbed they flew along the river, low over the water's surface, until lost to view. But this bird flew upwards towards the canopy of a dense woodland that covered many hectares. Almost immediately obscured, twisting in and out of the tree trunks, it was impossible to know whether it had turned left or right, and I was lost as to which direction to carry on searching.

In time I learnt more about this behaviour. As noted previously, when a dipper reaches the end of its territory, it simply does a U-turn and flies back the way it came. Kingfishers do not employ the same behaviour. If they are near the edge of their territory, they often fly *away* from the river and take a circuitous, semicircular flight path that ends up back at the river several hundred metres away. The problem for me was that, when hidden from view in a woodland, I could not discern in which direction the semicircle veered, so I was unable to search any further for the bird.

Interestingly, this behaviour provided a possible answer to a question that had often intrigued me. When I had encountered kingfishers in the past that had been killed striking windows, the house in question had often been located a reasonable distance from the river. Furthermore, sparrowhawks – the avian stealth hunter of the woodland – have often been cited as killing kingfishers. I had always thought of this as strange, even questionable, as I had never seen this woodland predator hunting low over a river. But the behaviour I had just witnessed for the first time provided an answer to both these mysteries.

I decided that I would walk closer to the willow, as there was no sign of the kingfisher in its bare branches. I had never seen it perched on previous occasions, but each time it had appeared to fly from the upper branches of the tree. As I tentatively approached, a kingfisher unexpectedly flew out from a low bough just below the edge of the bank and sped low across the river into an alder tree on the far side. It had not flown into the woodland canopy beyond, so I was hopeful of finally getting a view of it perched, and hopefully of ascertaining whether it was a male or a female. But no matter how carefully I scanned the bare branches of that tree, I failed to spot any colours other than those from a grey and green palette.

I stayed where I was, expecting the bird to make the next move. But, after twenty minutes with no further sightings, I realized that the bird must have somehow flown through the network of branches and tangled undergrowth and into the woods on the other side. Once again, I had fallen foul of the oldest of the magician's tricks: distraction.

The number of sightings centred around this willow tree were higher than random chance would suggest, especially as I rarely saw this bird elsewhere. There were clay banks on both sides of the river extending for about twenty metres in either direction from the willow. But these banks were very low and, at this time of year, only extended about half a metre above the river's surface. Heavy rain could easily raise the river level overnight, so that it would almost reach the top of the bank. Any nesting burrow excavated along this series of banks would not be safe until the early summer months, and, even then, perhaps not at all.

The water here was deep, but still fast-flowing. The depth of the water meant that no projecting rocks broke the mirrored surface, creating interference and disturbing the image of the riverbed below. This, I felt, was the attraction for the kingfisher. It was not searching for nesting sites; it had found a good fishing haunt. As I stood at the bank's edge looking into the water, I saw movement – there, below me, was a brown trout. Its intricately patterned back was a mosaic of differently sized black spots, each surrounded by a halo of white and set against a backdrop of beige.

Perfectly camouflaged, it blended into the pebble-strewn riverbed and was all but invisible. Only the swaying of its body, as it fought against the current, revealed its presence. Marvelling at its concealment, I had to remind myself that in reality it was not where it appeared to be. Had I tried to grab that fish I would have discovered that the refracted image was not where the actual fish hung suspended in the current. As I let my eyes roam across the glassy surface, other fish came in and out of focus: different sizes and colours, no two were the same. No wonder the kingfisher frequented here – it was a perfect hunting ground.

With the kingfisher now gone, I had to make a choice, and after some consideration I decided to carry on downstream. I had no way of knowing whether this feeding area was at the edge of a territory or in the middle. I would need to explore a kilometre of riverbank either side of this willow tree before I could hope to figure out that answer. As I made my way along the track running beside the river, it became more and more overgrown, forcing me away from the river's edge.

Rhododendrons, beautiful in gardens but highly invasive and damaging to our native woodlands, began to crowd out the bankside vegetation. Some stretches of river were all but impossible to see, and a kingfisher could easily remain hidden in the half-lit gloom of these Himalayan invaders. I found it depressing how these plants were becoming so prominent in the Wicklow Mountain landscape. Uncontrolled, they were as damaging as rats on an island preying on ground-nesting birds. All too often we encounter the same story with mankind. A lack of foresight and the planet suffers.

A clearing beckoned ahead, and the foreboding shade imposed by those dense shrubs was replaced by dappled light playing on a stardust-spangled river that danced its way through an open patch of young birch trees. I scanned the trees ahead, and in the last one, just before the river rounded the next bend, sat a kingfisher. Sunlight exploded off its plumage in a series of arcs, arches and rays made up of a spectrum of nothing but blue: cobalt, royal, Prussian, denim, powder, aquamarine, azure all radiated out from the glittering gemstone perched in front of me.

It sat there bobbing its head up and down and tilting its head, first to one side then the other, as it eyed up a fish below it. Then, taking off with a slight upward jump off the branch, it closed its wings tight against its body and plummeted towards the water. Travelling like an aerodynamic dart, it pierced the surface, the water offering no resistance, simply parting to allow the bird's entry. It disappeared in an explosion of water, columns of which erupted upwards and then outwards, before falling in a storm of droplets of ever-diminishing size.

The water continued to rain down, each droplet creating concentric ripples that grew, crashed and collided together, becoming interwoven. Then the kingfisher re-emerged, setting the sequence in motion again, only this time in reverse. Powering its body from the restraining grasp of the water, using its strong, round-shaped wings, it returned to its perch with a wriggling fish held firmly in its bill. The plumage of both sexes is identical, although the male sometimes appears more vivid and penetratingly coloured than its mate, especially if the pair are seen together. Despite this, given good views, it is relatively easy to tell the sexes apart by the colour of their dagger-shaped bills.

The male's bill is a solid black from base to tip. The female, on the other hand, displays a varying amount of pale colouration on the lower mandible, where it meets the feathers of the head: this can range from a subtle, pale grey to an almost-red pink. In good sunlight, using a telescope, this gleam of colour can be seen from a considerable distance. This bird's ebony-coloured bill, with no hint of paleness, told me it was a male. Possibly, like many other birds, the male had returned to the breeding territory ahead of the female to establish his claim to this part of the river – I hoped the female would follow shortly.

Holding the still-wriggling fish tightly, its head facing away from him, he smacked it several times off the branch on which he sat. Each time it wriggled less, until eventually it was still: dead or stunned, it made no difference now. Carefully manipulating the fish without letting it go, he turned it around so that he could swallow it headfirst. Doing so was an important task, as otherwise, if swallowed tail first, the fish's dorsal fin could snag in the bird's throat, possibly choking him.

Mastering the art of eating their food is a task young kingfishers must learn. Some fatalities in the first few weeks of their lives occur because they are unable to feed or dive successfully. Young birds have drowned or starved while learning to deal with the semi-aquatic habitat they live in. But those challenges had been met and successfully dealt with by this individual a long time ago, and, with the fish quickly swallowed, it set about the business of preening and keeping its diving suit in pristine order.

Using its bill, it took oil from a gland at the base of its tail and carefully worked it into each of its feathers to aid waterproofing. Neglect of this important task after each dive could lead to a bird's death. All birds need to maintain their feathers for different reasons, such as flight, warmth and courtship. But for kingfishers, and also dippers, continuous waterproofing of the feathers is of paramount importance. This is why they spend so much time preening, especially after they dive – it can take a long time to condition each of the many thousands of feathers on their bodies with oil.

Its preening attended to, the kingfisher glanced in my direction, then with a single whistle took off and disappeared down the river in a dazzling flash of electric blue. I proceeded to follow, but that was to be my final sighting of the day. Because it was still early spring, there was little growth on the riverbanks, and navigation along the water's edge was trouble-free. The forest of bracken, that later in the year would make the bank almost impassable, lay flattened by the earlier snow. This, coupled with the fact that the trees were mostly still bare, meant that I could easily scan a good distance ahead. But after a kilometre I admitted defeat and returned to the dippers.

During the preceding week, most of my observations of the dippers had only involved one bird, which, when I managed to examine it closely, had turned out to be the male. Unsure as to whether the female had been killed or had begun incubation, I returned to my aquatic exploration beneath the bridge. Kitted out as before with a lifejacket and safely secured by a rope, I waded my way against the strong current and through the deep central channel. Halfway across, a small, black shape flew out from the nest and disappeared upriver. Satisfied she was incubating, I returned to the bank and moved into the woodland. No sooner had I reached the shelter of the trees and turned around than I saw a dipper fly low along the river before flying up under the bridge and into the nest: incubation had definitely started. It is generally believed that only the female dipper incubates the eggs, although that is far from certain. It is usually impossible to identify the sex of a dipper in flight. Furthermore, when they reach the nest, they fly straight into the small entrance hole, without affording a chance to see which of the pair is involved. But ornithologists carrying out nest studies have usually only encountered the female in the nest, although there have been rare occasions when the male has been found in the nest.

Possibly the male briefly takes over once or twice a day to allow the female to feed, though I have never witnessed a changeover myself. The dense covering of moss on the outside of the nest must provide such good insulation that, when the female leaves the eggs unattended, there is little chance of them chilling before her return. During the days I watched the nest, I saw her leave on only a couple of occasions. She seemed quite content sitting for many hours with no involvement from the male.

The average clutch size for dippers is four eggs, and I have only seen the eggs on one occasion. A nest under another bridge was destroyed by an unknown predator several years ago. When I saw it, the domed structure had been partially ripped open, and much of the moss lay hanging like a torn shroud, exposing the woven structure within. It had not been the best-located of nests, built as it was on the wall of the bridge alongside the bank.

I suspected an American mink was the most likely culprit. An introduced species, escaping from fur farms in the 1950s, they wreak havoc on our native waterbirds and other wildlife. They represent yet another environmental disaster created by man's lack of understanding and negligence. Belonging to the same family as the otters I had encountered earlier in the year, for me they possessed none of the attractiveness or endearing qualities of that species.

Perhaps in their native land they do, but here they were neither welcome nor invited.

By making my way along the partly submerged ledge beside the bridge, I was able to examine the destroyed nest. There, inside the damaged structure, lay a single egg. Perhaps the attacker had been disturbed before eating all of them. The dipper's egg is a pristine white, as though carved from snow. The eggs of many cavity-nesting species are white too, but more of an off-white, cream or ivory shade – not the dazzling, immaculate and pure colour of the one before me. It was also a slightly unusual shape, being almost circular. However, it looked almost as though someone had slightly squeezed one side of the egg so that it protruded slightly, rather than being a perfect sphere.

Now that the female was sitting on the eggs, there was little gained by watching the nest. Hours could pass with no sighting of either bird. Even after a long wait, the only view I could expect was a brief glimpse in flight. A dipper incubates its eggs for an average of sixteen days, and only starts once the clutch is complete. When I realized that the female was remaining in the nest, I was pretty sure she had only been doing so for a couple of days. This meant it would be about a fortnight before I could expect any regular activity.

During this period, the male became very inactive and spent long periods simply standing on a stone at the river's edge, a hundred metres or so away from the nest. He looked lost without his companion by his side, which had been the case for many weeks. Occasionally he sang, especially on bright, sunny mornings, the loud, clear notes travelling well on the still air.

ONE DAY IN early April he stood at the edge of the bridge and sang alone. His bill pointed skywards while he held out his wings and fluttered them, his whole body trembling as though matching the exuberance of his vocalizations. I wondered if his mate, sitting above him in the dark, was the intended recipient of this performance, or whether perhaps an intruding male was present out of sight nearby ... unscientific, perhaps, but I favoured the former.

While the dippers were well underway with the business of rearing their family, the kingfishers had not even begun. Despite my pursuit of them, sightings were brief, inconsistent and extremely frustrating. Once, I had seen a female – identified due to the proximity of the bird, which allowed me to see the pale colouration on its bill. I now knew there was a pair along this river, but they seemed to have little interest in each other, and I never saw them together. Nor did I find any bank that I would have considered as a suitable nesting site, or even see them favouring a particular area.

The grey wagtails, however, while not as advanced in their breeding as the dippers, were far ahead of the kingfishers, and a nearby bankside was a flurry of activity from these feathered water nymphs. The male had spent the past month dancing along the shingle shoreline and performing twirling pirouettes in the sky as he sang and proclaimed his territory. Day after day he was a spectacular blaze of colour and activity.

His sulphur-coloured underparts glowed in the spring sunshine, while his black throat and white moustachial stripes positively shone. The slate-blue colour of his back gave him his name, but this colourful sprite was anything but grey. His long, black-and-white tail was rarely still, endlessly flicking up and down as he pranced along the shore. In flight he fanned and flashed it as he dipped and danced over the water's surface.

Over the past week he and his mate had been exploring a stretch of bank, hovering alongside it before disappearing in amongst the vegetation. Re-emerging, they would hover once more like a colourful pair of fairies before flying into a patch of grass or sprouting herbage. After many days of close examination and intense scrutiny, they had made their selection, and the pair was now busy gathering nest material.

Both birds partook in this, and I regularly saw them hopping about on the weed-covered rocks collecting large billfuls of suitable material. Unlike the dippers' complex construction or the kingfishers' extensive excavations, both of which take several weeks to build, a grey wagtail's nest is a far simpler affair.

A sturdy creation, constructed of grass stems, small twigs and mosses, surrounds a central cup lined with hair, fine grasses and occasionally a few feathers. Usually it takes less than a week to build, and sometimes it is completed within a few days. This pair had almost finished, and the dried stems and twiglets they had been carrying a day or two earlier were now replaced in their bills by tufts of hair. I suspected that a pair of horses not too far away were the most likely donors of this nest-lining material. Badger hair, snagged on low-lying branches or caught on wire fences, is also readily obtainable around this river, and I have often found it in old, disused nests.

Grey wagtails do not conceal their nests particularly well, and using my telescope I could clearly see part of the nest built against a tussock of sedge low down on the bank. If I could see it, I was sure a passing mink would have no trouble locating it too. But I had seen many nests like this over the years and they usually survived, so they obviously knew more than I did about choosing a suitable home for their family. By the time the dippers' incubation was nearing completion, the grey wagtails had finished their nest, laid their eggs and begun to incubate them.

Although it was easy to locate, I made no attempt to approach their nest site. However, in previous years I have often unexpectedly almost stood on a partially hidden nest. Without exception, all the nests I have seen contained four eggs or, later in the year, four chicks. I assumed this pair's nest was no different and contained four cream-coloured, pear-shaped eggs, covered with a dense spotting of reddish-brown. The female undertakes most of the incubation, but the male certainly contributes, unlike the dipper. It would now be a further twelve to fourteen days before the eggs hatched.

The Ides of March had come and gone, and both the wagtails and dippers sat tight, keeping their eggs warm. The kingfishers continued to elude me and settled into no pattern other than that of continuing with no pattern, for no purpose other than my frustration. As the days lengthened, the surrounding landscape responded with an outpouring of song: thrushes, finches, tits and wrens combined to fill the woodland and riverside hedgerow with music. Great spotted woodpeckers added some welcome percussion to the feathered orchestra, their resonant drumming carrying far across the river.

I only realized that the dippers' eggs had hatched when I started seeing dippers flying to and fro along the river with more frequency than I had in the previous few weeks. Because of their fondness of using bridges as nest sites, dippers are accustomed to people and not at all shy, so I was able to observe their comings and goings without the use of a hide or any other form of screening. Once I did not sit right beside the bridge, all was well.

The parents would either fly along the river and straight up into the nest, or they would land momentarily on a large boulder near the base of the bridge's arching walls, before flying into the nest. When the birds were newly hatched, the adults would fly up to the nest and go completely inside without a moment's hesitation. What went on within the nest was shielded from my eyes by a veil of moss. Most of the interesting observations came from simply watching their comings and goings and how they carried these out.

It quickly became apparent, within a day or two of hatching, that the two parents had very different approaches to feeding their youngsters. The female would leave the nest like a heat-seeking missile being dropped from a fighter plane. She simply dropped out of the nest like a stone, before orientating herself into flight and heading upstream, twisting and turning as she followed the contours of the riverscape. The male took a less dramatic approach. Having fed the young, he would drop onto the large boulder at the base of the bridge, where he would quickly preen himself. Then, with a loud *zit*, he would fly off in the opposite direction to her, downstream.

They also each had their own way of arriving to the nest, which was the exact reverse of their departure. The female would fly from further upstream back to the bridge, usually along the middle of the river. As she silently approached the bridge she would rise gracefully up, in a smooth curve, into the nest. Moments later she would relaunch herself from the nest and vanish upstream once again.

By comparison, the male would fly along the edge of the bank, calling to announce his arrival, and land on the boulder, which had now become his definitive property. After a few seconds he would then fly to the nest, sometimes hovering in front of it, before entering. Having fed the chicks, he would return to his marker stone before flying back downstream. While I occasionally saw the female near the rock, she never actually sat on it – that I saw, anyway.

I found it interesting that they each fed either side of the bridge, as though the nest was a dividing factor in their lives. The topography upriver from the bridge differed greatly from that below the river. Upstream, the watercourse was deep, and the water was hemmed in by banks heavily overgrown with dense and brooding rhododendrons. The female dipper had to fly several hundred metres along this dark, unwelcoming stretch of river before it opened out to include areas of shallow water, rippling and tinkling in the April sunshine.

The male travelled no distance at all, by comparison, and regularly fed along the river's edge within sight of the nest itself. Sometimes he was able to complete several visits to the nest with food in the time it took for her to complete one circuit. Perched on his rock, he provided me with opportunities to assess the size and quantity of food he was bringing to his chicks. In the initial days, the larvae he sourced were small and only barely visible in his bill. As the days passed, the size of the larvae he hunted would grow in accordance with the youngsters' ability to swallow larger prey items.

While I was able to make daily observations of the dippers, the same could not be said for the kingfishers. The advancement of the season had not presented any huge increase in sightings, and I was worried that I might fail to locate the nest at all. I began to realize that, although this stretch of the river was certainly within their range, it did not seem to be part of their core breeding territory. I would have to extend the search much further along the watercourse.

Unquestionably, this would involve more time, effort and commitment – quite an investment for a personal interest. A person unfamiliar with watching birds through direct observation in the field might perhaps struggle to understand the reasoning behind my determination. After all, kingfishers have been studied in great detail by scientists and photographers for many years. In today's world, where we can access 'instant information', there is no need to pursue lengthy field studies, especially where much of the information gathered consists of negative information or absence of data.

Furthermore, anyone watching animals on television, seeing them alive in the zoo or preserved in the museum could easily be misled into thinking there is little to be learnt. How wrong they are. I have always enjoyed looking closely at birds. Today, thanks to modern binoculars and telescopes, I can enjoy close-up details of birds' plumages that simply were not possible when I was growing up. Then, to see the intricate feather details I needed to look at birds in the Natural History Museum in Dublin.

FONDLY REFERRED TO today as the 'Dead Zoo', the museum is not at the top of the list of destinations that every birdwatcher wants to visit. Yet when I was a young birdwatcher, the Natural History Museum in Dublin was a central feature of my teenage years. It also provided me with my first close-up views of the kingfisher. Even more surprisingly, it enabled me to avoid playing rugby!

Having no interest in team sports was certainly a disadvantage for a pupil enrolled in a renowned rugby-playing school, where almost everyone else – and I mean almost *everybody* else – played rugby. Quite why I didn't like it, understand it or 'get it' was a source of constant puzzlement to my teachers, not to mention my classmates and even my parents. However, they tried to accommodate it in some manner, as they did with many aspects of my education, even though they failed to understand why I was so different.

'Well, he knows a lot about nature and wildlife,' my teachers would muse to my parents, and undoubtedly amongst themselves. During class they struggled to bring nature themes into the syllabus of English, history and even French. Hence, we discussed birdwatching as part of the oral French syllabus – to the utter disbelief, and sometimes scorn, of my classmates. While this may have helped me academically, it certainly didn't help me develop socially. The teachers lived in hope that the state exams would include a nature-themed poem by Thomas Grey or Thomas Kinsella, and that visiting examiners were prepared to discuss *migration des oiseaux*.

The problem with attending a sport-driven school was that one whole afternoon was given over to rugby training, which I didn't attend. Unlike many schools today, there was not a range of sporting options that might have provided a possible alternative: basically, rugby was compulsory. It was horrendous and torturous, and not just for me – the team was far from impressed that I was watching a sparrowhawk instead of the ball coming towards me. Mercifully, I was released from this torture thanks to the foresight of my mother, who wrote a letter to the headmaster asking that I be excused from rugby training, as it was causing me 'distress'. She was a most insightful lady.

So, what was I to do during this period of school? I could hardly be allowed to go birdwatching, catching butterflies or chasing frogs while other children were training in the art of chasing a ball across a field. A most unusual solution was provided by the Natural History Museum.

This Victorian-era building was one of my favourite destinations, after the zoo, to which my parents brought me month after month, until I was old enough to go by myself. It provided an opportunity to see the world of animals up close and brought my imagination alive, even though everything in the building was dead. Elephants, lions, tigers, bears – I became Willard Price, author of the many 'wildlife adventure books for boys' on my shelves, chasing through steamy jungles or Arctic wasteland in pursuit of his quarry, or Gerald Durrell capturing unknown animals from faraway lands and selling them to zoos. Here, surrounded by the smell of formaldehyde and tannin as I was, the creatures from those books became, in my mind, alive. I could touch the okapi or the mountain gorilla, in a manner more real than those seen distantly in the zoo.

Being such a regular visitor, I soon made acquaintances with the curators of the museum, who, recognizing my keenness, arranged for me to access the study collections of specimens in the research section of the museum. This appealed far more than rugby – or any other form of sport for that matter – and my school accepted another letter from my mother explaining that this was study worth being excused for.

And so, while the rest of the school played rugby each week, I travelled to the Natural History Museum and studied the natural world up close and in detail. Although all the animal kingdom was in effect made available to me, it was the bird section of the museum that really bewitched me. Birds known only from books and glimpsed on natural-history programmes could be seen up close, and in all their beauty. Exotic Mediterranean species such as hoopoes, their curved scimitar-shaped bills as bizarre-looking as their fabulous crests, reminiscent of a Native American chief's headdress. Bee-eaters, their bodies a crazy patchwork of clashing colours – rich chestnut, gold, turquoise, royal blue, yellow – almost as though an artist had simply let his or her imagination run loose with a full palette of colours. And of course there was the kingfisher.

Displayed in all its glory in a case of its own. A tastefully decorated display case with replications of water and bankside vegetation and two mounted birds, one hovering above the water, the other perched alongside a representation of its nest excavated in the side of a bank. Looking at these specimens up close, separated by only a sheet of glass, I was captivated by their size – they were so small, yet so exquisite in their colouring. Their iridescent feathers glittered every time I moved. Given their colouring, it was no wonder that a photograph of that kingfisher display featured on one of the postcards for sale in the museum. I still have one of the cards fixed into my nature diary from that period.

At the time, before digital cameras and the advanced optical equipment now used by most birdwatchers, examining mounted specimens in the hand was often the only way to see intricate plumage features on birds. As a young naturalist, the privilege of being allowed to wander, unsupervised and at will, amongst thousands and thousands of natural-history specimens on a weekly basis was a luxury then afforded to few people – and even more so today. The curators and scientists who worked there soon became used to this new face, who invariably knocked on their private study room doors each Wednesday afternoon, brimming with questions. After all, I had a whole week of learning to catch up on.

All those years I spent visiting the museum, and seeing birds such as the kingfisher in such fabulous, close-up detail, in no way lessened the joy I felt from seeing birds in the wild. However, I took those childhood memories, and others, with me and they accompanied me as I made my way along the riverbank.

EXPLORING FURTHER ALONG the river brought me into new aspects of the river habitat – around every bend was a surprise, a new world to be explored. As I made my way along the bank, an explosive series of loud quacks erupted from the low-growing vegetation at the water's edge. A male mallard, who had been hiding there as I approached, performed a spectacular, almost vertical take-off. The sunlight illuminated the myriad of droplets cascading from his orange, webbed feet, each one creating a rainbow that lived and died in a split-second. His head shimmered: one moment shades of bottle-green radiated from his plumage, the next an emperor's purple.

The mallard may be our most common and familiar species of duck, but the male is still a spectacular bird when viewed at close range. I watched him gain altitude, stretching his neck forward as he reached the treetops and banking right as he flew behind me, heading upstream. He was alone, but I knew that the female was most likely very close by and sitting tight on her nest. Perhaps, while flying away, his intense quacking had been a message for her to sit tight.

Mallard nests are usually well hidden, and I have often found them under bramble bushes along the riverbanks as well as much further from the water's edge. Sometimes on offshore islands I have found the nests many hundreds of metres from the sea. Not wanting to linger and risk disturbing the female, I quickly made my way along the bank.

Ahead of me was a grassy, muddy slope where sika deer had worn away the bank by using it to enter the water when crossing the river. A broken branch lay in the water, reaching out of the water like a cane, upon which sat a kingfisher. I quietly sat down, half-hidden amongst the willows, waiting and watching. It was the female, hunched up like a diminutive gnome. She sat quietly, unmoving, while the minutes passed. Then, without warning, the male arrived, landing beside her, standing proudly to attention with his bill pointing to a sky as blue as his crown. He greeted her with a loud whistling call as he proudly showed off his sleek, elegant profile. Throwing her head back, she opened her bill, not whistling but making a high-pitched, shrill plea. She held out her wings, adopting a submissive posture – but the male's response was to take off, and, calling loudly, he vanished around a bend in the river. The female took off and followed ... they were gone, but I knew they would return. The behaviour I had witnessed does not take place at any random point of a river. It was courtship behaviour, a prelude to mating, and as such usually occurred close to the chosen nest site ...

I had found the fishers' realm.

# THE RETURN OF
# THE CARPENTER

THE KINGFISHER WAS not the only bird found along the river that excavated a nest in which to raise its young. The great spotted woodpecker had been nesting in the oak woods that carpeted the sides of these valleys, through which I quested for several years. Formerly vagrants in Ireland, they first nested in County Wicklow in 2008. Their numbers slowly increased, year upon year, until their initial, tenacious hold on these woods became more steadied and permanent. I had followed the fortunes of one particular nest for many years, and fondly referred to the birds that nested there as the 'Spanish chestnut woodpeckers', due to their choice of nest site. Great spotted woodpeckers utilize a range of different tree species for their nests, oaks being the preferred choice in County Wicklow, but only one pair had ever selected a Spanish chestnut tree as their home – my pair.

Although by now the original colonizers who had made their initial carvings into the tree were undoubtedly deceased, a pair of woodpeckers had continued to nest in this tree each year since 2011. The tree itself was long dead; it was only a matter of time before its crumbling bole gave way and fell to the ground, continuing the cycle of life, death and rebirth. Until then, it was a high-rise woodpecker condominium.

Because of their unwavering faithfulness to this decaying monolith, I had built a wooden observation hide close by, just a few metres from the base of the Spanish chestnut itself. In previous years this had enabled me to enjoy close-up insights into the lives of these charismatic woodland birds. I had enjoyed watching intimate courtship behaviour, when the birds seemed truly unaware of anything other than each other. I had seen the first faltering wing flaps of a young woodpecker's maiden flight, while the parents watched with what I felt could only be admiration. And I had witnessed their deaths – cradling their tender bodies in my hands as their parents' hopes lay shattered before me. Their lifeless bodies, devoid of hope, resurrecting those feelings that every dead animal had brought to the surface since my childhood.

This was to be my seventh year watching this particular tree, and for many people must surely beg the question – why? After all, I had seen the birds excavate the nest hole and had spent countless hours watching them rearing their young. What was left to see? At its simplest, I watched because I enjoyed being part of their world – theirs and every other creature that shared it with me. There was always something new to learn, something I had never seen before, and this year there would definitely be something new to see – inside the nest.

Throughout the past years, I had been restricted to watching everything from the outside. The incubation of the eggs and the early development of the chicks had been a mystery, shrouded in the gloom of the twilight world they inhabited. Only when the chicks were two weeks old would they begin to appear at the entrance to the nest hole, at long last becoming visible to an outside observer. But so much had happened in the weeks prior to this, all details which had eluded me in previous years. How many eggs had been laid? What did they look like? How many chicks had hatched, and how many had survived until they reached the point where they were old enough to look out from their arboreal window on the world below?

The plumage of young woodpeckers differs from that of the adults in that the crown shows varying amounts of red. Adults have an all-black crown, although the male does have a deep-crimson patch on the nape of his neck, a feature that the female lacks. These varying amounts of colour on the crown act like a fingerprint: no two birds are marked the same. In the past, this has enabled me to work out how many young birds are in the nest. I could do this by comparing the patterns on their crowns when they each stretched their heads out to be fed by their parents. Although this often told me how many birds were in the nest that day, it did not tell me how many eggs had originally been laid, nor whether any chicks had died. To learn that, I needed to see into the nest hole, which meant I needed to see inside the tree itself.

Great spotted woodpeckers are often very individual birds, which is why I find them so enthralling. No two pairs behave identically. For the most part, they make their nests within a given range of variables involving, amongst others, species of tree, height above ground of the nest and the direction the nest hole faces. Most woodpeckers in Wicklow favour oak trees for nesting in, most nests face north and most entrance holes are situated between nine and twelve metres from the ground. But, as with human personalities, there is a whole spectrum of possibilities – I have seen some nest holes at eye level, whereas others are over twenty metres above ground, high in the crown of a towering conifer. The Spanish chestnut I had watched for so many years certainly had an entrance hole facing north – as well as ones facing east, south and west, with several attempts at points in between. And while oak was certainly a popular choice for nesting in, there were many other tree species used, as well as nest boxes and even a telegraph pole.

So, not every nest was going to be approachable with a view to looking inside – climbing to the top of a twenty-metre conifer was not on my to-do list, especially as I am terrified of heights and would most likely not even get to the top of the ladder to begin with. Fortunately, the woodpeckers that chose to use the Spanish chestnut as their home preferred a lower location for the siting of their nest. Over the years I had observed this tree, a total of five nest chambers had been excavated, different ones being used during different years, although some were used successively.

All were accessible using a long, two-section ladder. Naturally, being afraid of heights, I never had any intention of climbing up to

*The kingfisher is one of our most beautiful birds. Its upperparts, a chequer-board of dazzling shades of blue bedecked with glittering sequins, contrast with its warm orange underparts. It truly deserves its name of 'the jewel of the river'.*

*At a distance, dippers appear to be all black with a white throat. However, when seen close up the chocolate-coloured head and chestnut breast band reveal it to be a bird of surprising beauty.*

*Young dippers have a steel-grey plumage for the first few months of their lives.*

*This male great spotted woodpecker successfully raised his brood alone following the mysterious disappearance of his mate shortly after she laid her eggs. Photograph taken under licence by The National Parks and Wildlife Service © Declan Murphy.*

*Waiting patiently on a suitable perch overhanging the river, a female kingfisher watches for its prey.*

*Having caught its prey, the kingfisher must then turn it around to ensure that it swallows it headfirst.*

*Despite its brightly coloured plumage, the kingfisher can be hard to spot. Its small size and habit of sitting partially hidden by riverside vegetation means it often goes unnoticed.*

*A hunting kingfisher focuses intensely on its prey before making a spectacular dive. Kingfishers often sit motionless for long periods while waiting for a suitable opportunity to pounce.*

*A female grey wagtail is anything but grey, combining elegance with subtlety. Dancing and flitting over the water, they are ever active. Their elvish and impish activities make them the classic water sprite.*

*The male grey wagtail, identified by his black throat, is an attentive father, caring for his brood for many weeks after they leave the nest.*

*Shy, secretive and elusive, goosanders are one of our rarest breeding species of duck. Sculpted with sleek and flowing outlines, this male goosander is a beautiful sight on a mountainside river.*

*The shaggy crest on female goosanders gives them a distinctive wild and unkempt appearance. In Wicklow, goosanders are predominately restricted to fast-flowing rivers and mountain lakes in glaciated valleys.*

*At the first light of dawn, goosanders leave the mountain lakes where they spent the previous night and disperse throughout the network of nearby river valleys.*

*The female goosander cares for her large brood of youngsters alone, with no assistance from her mate.*

the top rung to measure entrance holes and gather other information – that unenviable task has been conducted over the years by one of my friends. While we have examined nest holes in previous years, during the winter months when the nests are not in use, it has always been an external examination. Measurements of the diameter of the entrance hole, calculations of the length of the entrance tunnel and estimations of the depth of the nesting chamber were all made using a piece of wire as a measuring tool. But the inside always eluded us.

But this season was going to be different, for I had finally procured an extendible, flexible CCTV camera. By inserting this into the nest hole we should hopefully be able to see the eggs and also the chicks when they hatched. Under the Wildlife Act 1976 (as amended in 2000) it is illegal in Ireland intentionally to disturb the nest of *any* wild bird without a licence. I therefore applied to the National Parks and Wildlife Service for permission to conduct this investigation. And so, as the storms of winter fought their final charge against the lengthening days, as the woods began to fill with birdsong and as the first spring flowers pushed through the woodland carpet of dead leaves, I stood ready – with camera and licence.

Whether looking for kingfishers or woodpeckers, there were always unexpected additional sightings and events that added to the day's enjoyment. As I approached a bend in the track along the river, I was suddenly hit by a wall of acrid, musky scent. It was so strong it was almost palpable in its warmth and undoubtedly tangible to taste, had I been so inclined.

I am always surprised at how few people are familiar with the scent of a fox, for that was the source of this highly quantifiable aroma. I have known for many years that I am extremely perceptive when it comes to smells and often find certain scents overwhelming, scents that others barely notice, if even at all.

A sense of smell is paramount to almost all mammals and many other animals. Yet in many humans it has been relegated to nothing more than a tool to be deployed in the kitchen or enjoyed in the garden. In the past, I have tracked down animals, plants, fungi and occasionally even people by scent alone, and today was no different. The invisible trail that hung in the air was so strong that I knew its owner was most likely still close by.

I dropped down into a crouched position behind a fallen tree and waited. Moments later, a fox emerged into view from a patch of dense undergrowth. I love watching foxes, and this one was a beauty. Its coat, gleaming with vitality and health, was fluffed up against the cool air, with each hair partially raised and separate from the others. The tail, like a thick muff, trailed down like an inverted question mark, culminating in a broad, white tip. The crisply delineated, orange-and-white fur was sharp in its colouration and unmarred.

But the picture was not perfect; the fox held a foreleg slightly raised and then tensed each time it touched the ground with the affected paw … it was lame. As I watched, it moved along the track, going away from me. Although hindered, it was by no means incapacitated, and out here in the woodlands I knew there was no assistance that I could offer it. Any animal in pain stirs me – not to pity, but with sympathy and understanding. However, the sight of that injured fox also stirred a memory: of another fox, another sore paw and a *very* perplexed veterinary surgeon.


FOR DECADES, James Herriot inspired many people to become vets with his series of entertaining books. I was no different in my romanticism, but academically I never stood a chance. The next best thing, to my mind, was to accompany a vet on his rounds. Thanks to a chance encounter, a local farm vet was kind enough to allow me to accompany him each Saturday. It was a wonderful opportunity to see the world of large-animal medicine up close, which I continued to enjoy for several years. For me, it ranked as equal in stature with my unique experiences in the Natural History Museum.

Early on one of those Saturday mornings, as we drove down a country road, a fox hopped down from a wall and began to cross the road. 'Stop!' I shouted out, as I realized the animal in front of us was limping.

'Look, it's hurt,' I said, turning to the driver.

He smiled at me, saying, 'Yes, but I'm sure it will be OK, it's only a fox.'

Without thinking any further, I opened the door of the car, jumped out and ran down the road after the stricken creature.

The fox took one look at my approaching figure and bolted down a driveway towards a gate, which, unfortunately for it, was a dead end. When it realized its mistake and turned to go back the way it had come, I had reached the top of the driveway, effectively cutting off its escape. We stood there facing each other, as though we were antagonists, while I tried to think of what to do next ... I quickly took off my coat and, with little rational thought, ran at the fox and threw the coat over the startled animal.

Somehow, through the coat, I managed to hold the back of its neck with one hand while holding its rump with the other. Carrying the frightened, hissing and violently struggling animal with me, I returned to my friend's car. There is no word to describe the look on that poor vet's face as I approached with my squirming trophy held at arm's-length. 'Look,' I shouted triumphantly, 'I caught him!'

He stared at me in disbelief, his jaw wide open. Then, composing himself, he asked, 'And *what*, exactly, are you planning to do now? Because that fox is *not* coming into this car with us.'

My reply, simple and uncomplicated, left my poor friend speechless. 'He's hurt,' I said, 'and you're a vet ...'

Fortunately, it was only a minor injury to one of the fox's claws which caused the lameness. We treated him there on the side of the road, and when I finally let him go in a nearby field, he galloped away with neither a limp nor a backward glance. Getting back into his car, the vet, my senior by many years, looked at me and said, 'Let's keep this to ourselves, OK?'

IT MAY HAVE been spring according to both the calendar and the cycles of life, but it was still cold and grey – very cold and grey. Above me, the sky was the colour of the linseed putty my father used to bed glass into window frames, grey with a hint of purple. The bare branches of the oaks overhead, black against that insipid backdrop, criss-crossed like a drunken spider's web, their chaotic patterns creating a bizarre explosion of images in my mind. Not a single leaf was visible on those trees, for the oak is usually the last of our native trees to emerge from its winter sleep.

I was standing alongside the river, a hundred metres or so from where I had witnessed the pair of kingfishers performing the early stages of their courtship. I had not managed any sightings of them that morning, despite searching both upstream and downstream from where I stood. The fact that the river was still engorged with recent rain was most likely the reason for their absence. The churning brown water, bedecked with crazily hurtling blocks of foam, thundered past me. It would be a brave or foolhardy bird which would attempt diving into such torrents.

In front of me was a male grey wagtail, standing on a large boulder jutting out from the bank into the turbulent waters. He had a billful of moss, which he had been carefully picking off from the rock on which he was perched. The moss would be used as nesting material for the cup-shaped nest in which the red-speckled, white eggs would be laid. He stood there watching me, bobbing his long tail up and down, reluctant to leave, as to do so would draw attention to his chosen nest site.

This was a different territory to the one further upstream near the dippers. Unusually, this stretch of the river was home to three pairs of dippers in close proximity to each other. In most river habitats the territories are spaced out, and rarely do pairs meet. However, this river was a rich feeding ground, resulting in a higher density than normal.

As I watched him, a familiar sound emanated from the oak trees behind me. Impossible to transcribe, it was best described as a sudden burst of staccato, like a drum roll on a wooden percussion box; it was, of course, a great spotted woodpecker. In most species of bird, the male defends a territory, in which he and his mate will rear their family. The chosen territory is proclaimed by a variety of methods, including display and song.

Birds such as the robin sing from a prominent song post, marking it as one of the boundaries of their territories. We categorize many birds as 'songbirds' because of our interpretation of their songs as something beautiful and pleasurable. But to the birds involved they are merely warnings to other birds that this territory is occupied, coupled with a warning to stay away. Woodpeckers are not 'songbirds'. They do not sing to proclaim a territory – they drum.

'Drumming' is the term given to the sound made by a woodpecker when it strikes a branch with its bill in rapid succession. Although predominantly conducted by the male, the female often partakes too, resulting in a drumming duet, an enchanting experience, beautifully orchestrated against a woodland backdrop. When drumming, the bird will strike the wood at up to fourteen times *per second*. Each burst usually lasts between two and three seconds. Depending on the resonance of the chosen branch, and whether it is alive or dead, the sound can travel for up to a kilometre, reverberating out across the glades and through the trees, before fading away into silence.

Apart from this distinctive sound, usually only performed in the late winter and early spring, great spotted woodpeckers make several distinctive calls. The first, and most frequently heard, is a loud, strident *PIK*. Usually this is given as an alarm call, warning of a person's presence or if a predator has been spotted in the immediate vicinity. Unlike the drumming, woodpeckers call throughout the year, as circumstances dictate. The other sound I frequently hear is a 'rattle'. This particular sound is only made by a mated pair and seems to be a bonding exercise, strengthening their commitment and resolve to mate and successfully raise a family.

I scanned the tops of the trees with my binoculars until I found the source of the wooden-sounding drum roll. He was clinging upside down to a dead spur jutting off the main trunk. Holding on with his claws, while bracing his strongly reinforced tail feathers against the wood to steady himself, he continued to beat out his tattoo as I watched. Then, with a couple of loud *Pik … Pik* calls, he flew off deeper into the woodland. His distinctive bounding flight always reminded me of the sine waves I had struggled to understand in school. He had flown in the direction of the dead Spanish chestnut: it seemed that this year the tree would once again play host to this charismatic species. Each year had provided further insights into this recent colonist from Britain, and I expected the coming year to be no different; in that, I was proved correct.

My eyes greeted the dawn as the first arc of the sun climbed over the distant horizon, casting shafts of light over the sleeping landscape. Tendrils of mist rose from the frozen countryside as the weak warmth of the growing light caused the frost to begin its retreat. Woodpeckers are not the earliest of risers, but I wanted to be in the woods by the time the birds began their daily activity.

On my arrival at the glade surrounding the solitary Spanish chestnut, I was welcomed by a piercing *PIK* as a black-and-white bullet sped away from the tree. No doubt about it, they were intent on nesting in the same tree. A quick examination revealed neither a new nest hole nor any recent excavations. Satisfied, I went into my nearby observation hide, located several metres away from the base of the tree.

Made from rough-hewn wooden planks, the hide kept me shielded from the elements as well as the relentless onslaught of the Wicklow biting midges, which would infest these woods in the coming months. Hidden from the woodpeckers' keen eyesight, I was able to enjoy a close-up and intimate portrait of their daily lives.

Because of this rather hastily built structure, I have, over the successive seasons, been able comfortably to carry out observations in rain, snow and hail, as well as sunshine. I had seen so many aspects of the woodpeckers' lives play out on this tree: courting, mating and raising their young – as well as witnessing that pivotal moment when their chicks took those first faltering flaps into the woodland realm that awaited them.

Patiently I watched the trees in front of me through the small windows I had cut in the planks. The glade was quiet, apart from the sound of a distant mistle thrush singing; its wild, desolate and ringing tones spoke of loneliness, of solitude and of wildness. Alone in the woodland, the lonesomeness of the thrush's notes seeped into my soul like coldness penetrating the body.

Without warning, a woodpecker alighted on the tree in front of me, the crimson spot on the back of its head readily identifying it as a male. Its relaxed demeanour as it perched on the tree, and the absence of any call, showed me it was unaware of my presence. After a few moments he hopped further up the tree and onto a small branch, where he started drumming. When people hear a woodpecker's drumming, more often than not the bird is some distance away, high up in the crown of a tree. Although loud and distinctive, it would not be described, by most, as spectacular.

However, for me, the experience was totally different. With the bird perched only metres from me, the sound was ear-splitting. What is more, its proximity meant I not only heard it, but I felt it – or so I imagined. The sound seemed to travel from the branch, down the fungi-covered bole of the tree and into the roots, the intricate web of which integrated the various aspects of the woodland realm into one.

Dispersing across the glade, it passed through me like an ocean wave, resonating through my body and permeating every living thing as far as sound can travel. This was not a sound *from* the woodland – this was the voice *of* the woodland.

The sun had now climbed above the hills to the east of the woods, and the first rays of the early spring sun touched the tree and lit up the woodpecker, as though an amber spotlight had been positioned above him. He stopped his drumming and began preening; his smart, black-and-white plumage shone in the light, and the scarlet patch on his head and under his tail glowed – he was radiant.

With a throaty chuckling sound, he greeted his mate as she flew onto the tree from the nearby crown of a towering beech. Other than the absence of a red patch on the back of her neck, both birds were identical in appearance. The couple sat alongside each other, the female half-closing her eyes. The male carried on tending to his plumage before turning around and gently preening the feathers on the back of his mate's head. This mutual grooming strengthens the bond between them.

I was intrigued by their lackadaisical attitude towards the oncoming nesting season – seemingly no stress or worries bothered them. If they had been planning to excavate a new nesting chamber, I would have expected them to be busy doing so by now, as it can take several weeks for the pair to carve out the nest inside the tree. Most likely they had chosen to use one of the previous nest holes; but which one? During past seasons they had made nest holes on all sides of the tree – but my hide only faced one side. In the past two years I had been lucky, and both their choices had been visible from my hide; would my luck hold again this year?

As this tree was located only a short distance from the river, I was able to visit it regularly as I continued my search and observations of kingfishers. The woodpeckers continued to work their magic, and rarely more than a day or two passed without the glade calling out to me. Their attention was focused on the same nest hole they had used the preceding year, and there was no sign of any new excavations by early April.

Several times, as I had watched from the hide, the female had hopped up to the hole and stuck her head inside, as though checking all was well. However, I had also seen her checking out two of the other holes, including one on the far side of the tree. That, I felt, was not a positive development.

Until the eggs are laid in late April, there is often little activity to be seen around the nest, and several hours can pass without any sightings of woodpeckers. Occasional bursts of drumming and sporadic *Pik* calls are often the only indication that they are still around. By mid-April I had seen the female go into the nest hole facing the hide on several occasions, so apparently the choice had been made.

Often while inside the nest, she would come up to the entrance and stick her head out and look around. Minutes would pass with her sitting there, often looking straight towards me, unbeknownst to her. What was she thinking? I often wondered. Given that her brain is only the size of a walnut, it is easy for humans with their advanced cognitive powers to say she was thinking of nothing. But, time and time again, some birds and animals have shown signs of empathy – certainly not as advanced as our human empathic responses, but a capacity for feelings nonetheless. Perhaps, as she sat there watching me, she was missing the presence of her mate, or was simply enjoying the sights, sounds and scents of that early spring morning, exactly as I was.

BY MID-APRIL I began to wonder whether the eggs would be laid during the coming week. In order to get the date of the first egg being laid, I would need to check the nest every three days. Like most birds, woodpeckers lay a single egg each day until the clutch is complete. What, or who, dictates the size of the clutch exactly is unknown. In England, great spotted woodpeckers usually lay between five and seven eggs, but was Ireland any different?

I arrived at the glade on 20 April with a ladder, camera and, most importantly (since, as we have already established, I had no head for heights whatsoever), a companion to scale the tree for me. Because of undulations in the ground, even apparently low nests can still be quite high and hard to access. This nest was almost ten metres above ground, and even a large, two-stage ladder, when positioned against the tree, fell well short of the entrance hole.

Once the ladder was in place, my friend climbed to the top rung and securely lashed the ladder to the tree using a ratchet strap. Then, balancing precariously, he was just about able to reach up to the hole. Climbing up the ladder below him, and without looking down, I nervously passed the camera up to him and watched as he poised unsteadily on the narrow metal step. We would have presented a most bizarre sight to anyone passing by.

Slowly he began feeding the flexible cable up and into the nest hole. Trying to get the camera into a position where we could see the bottom of the nest chamber proved challenging and immensely frustrating. The cable transmitting the image could be bent into any shape. We needed to extend it straight up, then make a right-angle bend as it entered the tree, followed by another right-hand bend as it worked its way down along the walls of the chamber.

This resulted in creating an inverted U-shape, which then had to be manipulated into the tree by my friend as he balanced awkwardly almost ten metres above the ground. Eventually we had a reasonable length of cable inside the tree and turned on the attached LED lights, illuminating the inside of the chamber. Because my friend was unable to see the screen and manipulate the camera at the same time, I ascended further up the ladder until I could see the screen on the hand-held unit.

Those first images from inside an Irish great spotted woodpeckers' nest caught me completely by surprise. I had always assumed, from the neatness and preciseness of the chiselled entrance hole, that the chamber itself would be perfectly shaped and smoothly carved. I was wrong. The walls were fissured with cracks, gullies and crevasse-like features.

It was extremely hard to guide the camera from outside the tree. It wedged itself first into one wall, before twisting awkwardly around and getting stuck on the other side. It was enormously challenging to ascertain direction, and we even managed to look back up towards the entrance hole instead of deeper into the tree. What we saw was a chaotic assembly of images, many of which looked not unlike a close-up of the planet Mercury. This then was no expertly carved chamber.

I realized from the images that the centre of the tree was rotten and hollow. The woodpeckers had tunnelled into a ready-made cavity already existing inside the tree, hidden from the outside world. The cavity didn't run vertically as I would have expected a properly excavated chamber to do. It was angled at forty-five degrees, slanting back towards the same side as the entrance hole. This made it even harder to guide the camera towards the bottom of the chamber – wherever that may have been.

I provided whatever help I could from my perch below. 'No, that's facing up, I can see the hole … No, I can just see the wall, you need to angle it downwards … No, that's worse, try turning it the other … WAIT – THERE!' I shouted.

I could scarcely believe my eyes as a group of white, semicircular objects swam into view. There was not just one egg in the nest, there were six. Arranged in a circular pattern, each one evenly spaced from the other and positioned so that there was a small hole in the centre of the pattern, like a Polo mint. Although oblong in shape, they were not exceptionally pointed at either end, meaning they were not the classic, oblong egg shape of most other birds.

They appeared to be glossy white, with no markings of any type: the eggs of many hole-nesting birds are white, the theory being that this makes it easier for the birds to see their eggs in the near-darkness of the nesting cavity.

I was always fascinated by eggs as a young naturalist. Egg-collecting was quite popular with older generations of birdwatchers, but is now completely illegal under the Wildlife Act 1976 (as amended 2000). However, it is not illegal to collect discarded eggshells, from which the chicks have hatched, from beneath a nest. Being a skilled observer, I enjoyed the challenge of finding birds' nests and watching them from a safe distance.

By the time I was in my early teens I had amassed a considerable variety of eggshells, all of which were lovingly kept in boxes lined with cotton wool and labelled with the date and location I found them. The mottled, green-and-brown eggs of blackbirds sat alongside the small, sky-blue miniature 'cups' of dunnocks. But my collection was not just confined to garden birds: moorhens, pheasants, mallards and even great black-backed gulls were all represented in the growing number of boxes under my bed.

During the winter months I often collected old and disused nests from the bare, windswept hedges. Like the eggshells, studying these wonderful creations was a great way to learn more about birds. The nests of the blackbird and the song thrush were easy enough to find, but it took perseverance to find the smaller, fragile constructions of the finch and even the goldcrest. Quite often an infertile egg remained in the nest, providing me with a 'perfect' egg – a real prize when compared to the broken fragments that more typically occupied my matchboxes.

Nowadays, few birdwatchers collect old nests or eggshells, and the simple pleasure of engaging with nature at this level is relegated to schoolchildren collecting for 'the nature table'. Why we encourage this engagement so enthusiastically at that age and deem it irrelevant at all later stages of life is a mystery to me.

Despite my extensive experience with eggs, I had never encountered any quite like these woodpecker eggs. Their strange, oblong shape and roundness at both ends made them unlike any I had seen before.

Now that we knew there were eggs in the woodpeckers' nest, it was time to go and let the birds return to the job of caring for them. We untied the ladder and climbed back down, before quickly moving all the equipment away from the tree and out of view. We slipped into the hide and watched the tree; silence descended upon that part of the woods.

A few minutes later, the male landed on the tree. He perched on the edge of the entrance hole, his feet half inside the tree and half outside. His strong, reinforced tail feathers were pressed against the bark below him and splayed outwards, showing the sharply pointed tip to each feather. His head and body were angled away from the tree, his weight supported by his tail and claws.

He sat there motionless, a perfect sculpture in silhouette. I was so close that, using my binoculars, I could see the pupil of his eye glistening as he scanned the surrounding woods. Satisfied that there were no threats, he squeezed his body through the entrance hole and into the tree to begin incubating the eggs. I did not think it strange, at the time, that it was the male who returned to brood the eggs, since both parents shared the family duties between them.

Seeing those eggs inside the tree made me feel privileged. As far as I was aware, no other person had ever seen inside an Irish woodpeckers' nest, let alone seen the eggs inside a tree. From the observations I had been making, I was fairly confident that the final egg had been laid by the female only that day, or possibly the day before. Like most birds, she would have deposited a single egg each day during the preceding week, and incubation only started on completion of the clutch.

The following morning, I arrived at the nest; no woodpecker heralded my arrival with a warning call. Presumably one parent was incubating while the other foraged for food nearby. Nevertheless, I would have expected to have been observed making my way past the nest. I went into my hide and started to unpack my rucksack, setting myself up for the day. It was cold that morning, and although I was wearing a hat, gloves and scarf, the first thing on my mind was my flask and a cup of coffee – after all, it was going to be a long day, so I might as well be comfortable.

Having a coffee in my woodland has become a bit of a ritual and takes some preparation, as all good rituals do. I took out my cafetière and poured some hot water from my flask into it. While it was warming, I selected my ground coffee – I usually bring several types to match my mood through the day. Java coffee is strong – too strong, unless it's the end of a long day and I'm in danger of falling asleep, something which has happened in the past. My Costa Rican blend also had a strong kick, so I chose my morning favourite, a Blue Mountain blend, which was mellow and chocolatey with a hint of vanilla.

Looking out at the nest hole there was still no sign of either woodpecker, so I returned to my brewing enterprise. I threw out the water from the cafetière and added in four measures of ground coffee, before topping up with hot water and leaving it to infuse. Rummaging in my rucksack, I found my packet of Hobnobs – the sandwiches could wait. Finally the coffee was ready, and, having poured myself a cup and opened the packet of biscuits, I closed my eyes and leaned back against the wooden wall of my hide.

The smell of the coffee mingled with the other woodland scents. The rich and fruity aroma of the damp leaf litter and humus were like a plum pudding. The sharp, acrid scent of the bruised woodland flowers I had walked over filled my nostrils: wild garlic, Jack-by-the-hedge, wood anemone and nettle – I knew them all, and their welcome woodland incense filled my nostrils. The sweet smell of the freshly emerged leaves on the nearby beech trees added a final top note to this woodland perfume.

I did not need to open my eyes to see this world around me; my other senses told me everything I needed to know. Birdsong filled the air and the chorus, which to many people appears as a unified orchestra, filtered into my ears as individual strands of sound. It emanated from every direction and from a multitude of performers. Blackbird, song thrush, mistle thrush, dunnock, robin, wren, blue tit and treecreeper all filled the air with their territorial announcements. Each, for me, was as recognizable and individual as the voices of my own friends or siblings.

Half a packet of Hobnobs and an empty mug later, I opened my eyes – I still had not heard a single call from a great spotted woodpecker. I watched the tree in front of me for signs of activity, but nothing moved. An hour passed and still no woodpecker called or showed itself. I knew there were eggs, I knew there were two birds and I knew they were incubating; so, what was going on?

In previous years the birds took turns to incubate the eggs, swapping roles roughly every thirty minutes. As the foraging bird approached the nest, it often called to let the incubating bird know it was coming. Landing beside the nest hole, the bird inside the tree would then fly out, allowing the other to take its place. It normally happened like clockwork, and had done so every other year ... but not today.

As the second hour passed with a similar lack of activity, I decided on a new tactic: I picked up a stone from beside my feet and tapped it rapidly and firmly against one of the timber uprights that supported my hide. Although I could not strike the wood at fourteen times a second, in the manner of a woodpecker, the tapping I created did sound a bit like the sounds a feeding woodpecker makes.

I watched the nest hole as I made the tapping, and to my amazement a head appeared and peered out. Stretching its neck out, long and sinuous, the bird craned its head from side to side as it searched for the source of the sound. It looked like a cobra swaying and twisting in front of me. As it turned its head I could clearly see the scarlet on its nape: this, then, was the male.

At least I knew the eggs were still being incubated. But, in all the years I had watched woodpecker nests, I had never encountered such a length of time without a pair changing places. The male great spotted woodpecker usually does more than his fair share of work, and regularly carries out about 60 to 70 per cent of the family-rearing duties. Nevertheless, the female should have been back by now.

After a few moments, he withdrew back inside the tree to continue sitting on the eggs, and I settled back onto my seat to continue watching. Then, after a further half-hour, came a bigger surprise. Without warning, the male suddenly flew out of the nest and into the canopy above him – leaving the eggs unguarded. While this would not be unusual with some other species of birds, it was extremely out of character for this one.

I watched him hopping along a branch near the top of a bare oak. He was feeding in an unusually frantic manner as bits of lichen-covered bark and small pieces of wood rained down on the woodland floor. In between bursts of frenzied feeding he furiously preened himself. Sitting inside a cramped tree cavity for long periods was obviously quite taxing. He carried on with his ablutions and foraging for about ten minutes. During this time, he remained in the glade surrounding the nest, not disappearing deeper into the woods as in previous years. Then, without a single call, he glided down from the treetops on outstretched wings and silently slipped back inside the tree.

I had never seen this behaviour before. His actions seemed to indicate he was alone: long periods inside the tree, no changeover and not going too far away from the nest when foraging. But although it may have looked like he was alone, I felt there was more to this. There had to be a female around – there were six eggs in the nest, after all, and the last one had possibly been laid as recently as the preceding day. I had also seen her several days previously with the male. So where was she?

I continued my vigil as the sun climbed, reached its zenith and commenced its descent. The changing aspect of the sun throughout the day was mirrored in the changing tones of light that played across the glade. Shadows moving, hiding, reappearing and merging as the blue sky overhead lightened, bleached and darkened in accordance with the passing of the day. Inside my hide the flask emptied, and packaged food was replaced with empty wrappers and crumbs – even the Java coffee was gone. And through all of this, the male woodpecker kept his own vigil.

Instead of the clockwork changeovers every thirty minutes or so, as in previous years, hours now passed between his brief emergences. There was no pattern to his behaviour, and I often felt that he only came out when he could no longer tolerate the endless sitting inside the tree. As the day began to draw to a close, there had still been no sign of the female, and the male's new behaviour had remained consistent throughout. I now realized that this year was going to be very different to all my previous ones spent watching this nest. Not just had I seen the eggs inside the tree for the first time – I now had a single-parent family.

I found it hard to believe that the female woodpecker had laid her sixth egg and then died or been killed, yet that is what happened. Great spotted woodpeckers have few predators, but those they do have are formidable – as well as beautiful. Pine martens, known in Irish as *Cat Crainn*, or 'tree cat', are well able to climb any of the trees this pair of woodpeckers frequented.

However, although pine martens were increasingly predating nests and killing the chicks by ripping out the nest, it was rare for them to catch an adult bird. Several years ago, I did find a female great spotted woodpecker freshly killed by a pine marten, but it seems to be a rare occurrence. In that particular case I think the female may have been foraging on the ground when the pine marten pounced on her.

The sparrowhawk, an apex predator of deciduous woodlands such as this, is well able to catch a variety of birds in mid-air, and a woodpecker would pose no trouble to this fast-flying raptor. Given the time of year, when the birds were actively flying around in bare treetops, I felt that the sparrowhawk was the most likely culprit. However, despite all my hours of observations, I would never know for certain what had happened to her – some things remain unresolved.

What I did know was that there were six eggs in a tree in front of me, being cared for solely by one bird. It is not unusual for some species of birds, such as phalaropes, to entrust the incubation and rearing of chicks to the father, but I had never heard of woodpeckers deliberately doing this. Furthermore, even after hatching, the rearing of the youngsters takes longer than that of most other woodland birds – over three weeks, in fact.

OVER THE YEARS I have watched these birds, I have come to realize that the family life of the great spotted woodpecker demands a huge commitment of resources from both parents. I was uncertain whether the male could manage both the incubation and the rearing of the chicks by himself. Several years before, I had found a nest in which the male bird had died a week or so after the eggs had hatched. The female did her best and continued to feed the growing youngsters, but she was unsuccessful, and the nest failed.

Since the male often seems more 'committed' than the female, or certainly more involved, I felt that perhaps a male could succeed where a female had failed. But incubating six eggs for almost two weeks, followed by over three weeks feeding six hungry mouths inside the nest, before finally caring for them outside the nest for another two weeks was an incredibly challenging task … I wondered if he could possibly do it?

Meanwhile, as the male woodpecker began his lonesome vigil inside the tree, the kingfishers continued with their riverside courtship.

That earlier sighting I had enjoyed, of the two kingfishers posturing and displaying, had filled me with a great sense of satisfaction. Unlike other sightings further upstream near the dipper family, which were most likely unrelated to breeding, the sight of this pair together was far more encouraging. Like the woodpeckers sitting on the Spanish chestnut tree and preening each other, I felt that the kingfishers would most likely only sit around like this in the vicinity of their chosen nest site. However, whether the nest itself was excavated or not was another question.

I embarked on my search with renewed vigour throughout the following week. However, my enthusiasm was not matched by that of the weather. One morning, after several days of fruitless searching, my eyes were met by an unwelcoming grey sky. A persistent, fine drizzle descended from a low-lying cloud and continued for much of the day. Gathering on the leaves of the surrounding trees, it painted them with a transparent, shiny veil, culminating in a single, pearl-shaped droplet on the tip of each leaf. As short-lived as the shattered filaments of a waking dream, each droplet rolled off and extinguished itself on the ground below.

I walked the rain-sodden banks for a kilometre in both directions from where I had seen the pair of kingfishers. Further downstream, a pair of dippers bobbed in tandem on the rocks and foraged in the rushing water as they gathered food for their chicks, located nearby in an as-yet-undiscovered nest. But apart from them, and a male grey wagtail prancing along the water's edge, nothing caught my eye along this stretch of the river; no blazing, blue flash struck my eyes.

Much of being a naturalist involves patience, and long hours of what may seem to the uninitiated as 'nothingness'. For me, the time spent looking and searching for any animal or plant is only part of the experience; the immersion of oneself in nature and its surroundings, and the indulgence of the senses, is the reward for effort. I feel sorry for people who search unsuccessfully for a particular aspect of nature and feel the time was wasted.

Over the following week I explored this new stretch of the river, and eventually I discovered that the kingfishers favoured a stretch almost a kilometre in length, most of which flowed through oak woodland. It was a continuation of the same woodland where the lone male great spotted woodpecker was struggling to raise his family. This entire distance of water looked suitable for them to use for breeding. Although some of it was rocky, with occasional rapids, much of it was slow-flowing, with deep pools that reflected the overhead clouds.

Many of these pools had overhanging white willow and alder trees, providing feeding perches and cover for the secretive fisher. The open clay faces of the riverbank near these pools looked perfect for the kingfisher to tunnel into and excavate a nesting chamber. But no nesting chamber was visible on any of the banks I examined, nor indeed any kingfisher. Every time I saw the pair, either alone or together, I would search the adjacent banks for any signs of their nesting activity, but always I drew a blank.

Several days later I was walking downstream from where I had recorded my first sighting of the pair together. The water along this stretch had mellowed from its racing, chaotic and expressive journey to a deeper, almost thoughtful passage along exposed clay banks and dark, reflective pools shaded by dense overhead vegetation. Lost in my own racing, chaotic thoughts randomly arriving from every direction – except the right one – I was startled by an explosion of orange, then blue, and finally azure, as a kingfisher exploded out from the bankside below me and flew off.

Lying down on my belly, I examined the bank below me. Like the numerous other clay bank faces I had examined, this one looked suitable: not too stony, and with plenty of suitable-looking perches in the vicinity. Yet, as with all the others I had examined, there was no sign of any excavations, either past or present. I was totally perplexed. Why were these birds proving so difficult to study? What was I missing?

I continued searching that day until the sky started to turn a dark, velvety blue, its depth deepening as it arched eastwards over my head. Streaks of gold from the long-set sun painted random patterns across the heavens, but I failed to see the kingfisher again, nor did I find any

# WHIRLPOOLS AND EDDIES

LIKE A SERIES of waves, spring advanced ceaselessly northwards. A relentless surge of life was emerging and responding to a call it could not comprehend, yet one it was compelled to follow. The first swallows had returned from Africa and skimmed low over the river, their lively, twittering song a harbinger of the summer to come. Under the bridge, the dippers continued to tend to their rapidly growing family.

It takes over three weeks from the date of hatching before young dippers leave the nest. By comparison, the young of the similarly sized blackbird, one of our most common garden birds, leave the nest after less than two weeks. The youngsters, hidden in their nest located in the shadowy recesses of the bridge, had now been tended to by their parents for over a fortnight. Being as they were unperturbed by people, it was quite easy to watch the birds without the need for a hide, once I did not position myself too close to the nest.

Often I watched them by simply lying on my belly, half-hidden in the rapidly thickening bankside vegetation. They would sometimes feed within metres of me, their heads submerged beneath the water as they probed amongst the stones for their prey. Once they had gathered as much as they could carry, they would fly back to the nest to feed their demanding family. As the chicks approached their final week in the nest, the parents were visiting the nest on average once every four minutes.

Although I could not see the young birds, I could certainly hear them. As soon as a parent bird flew up to the nest, a rowdy chattering erupted from within: *zit-zit-zit-zit-zit*. With each passing day, as the young birds grew larger and stronger, the sound increased in volume and intensity. When the parent bird left, the noise continued for up to a minute before gradually stopping.

Most species of bird practise good house hygiene within the nest. Usually when a parent bird brings food to its young, it removes any faeces that they have produced. I have seen woodpeckers, thrushes and tits all diligently carrying these unwanted parcels away from the nest, but never dippers. When a dipper chick needs to defecate, it simply positions itself at the entrance hole of the nest, so that the excrement drops into the water below.

Because of this, adult dippers do not enter the nest in the same manner as the great spotted woodpecker when feeding the chicks. They fly up to the nest and either land, clinging to the outside of the nest, or sometimes just hover like helicopters in front of it. They quickly thrust the food into the gaping mouths of the youngsters, which stretch their necks outward from the nest, before flying off to gather more food. Of course, all this riotous begging from the youngsters poses the risk of attracting unwanted attention. In nature, there is always something that wants to eat you.

The alarm call of the male dipper was far louder than normal. *ZIT-ZIT*, he called as he flew agitatedly from bank to bank. Looking beyond him, further downstream I glimpsed something slender, black and fast-moving amongst the tangled brambles along the bank. My initial thought was that it must be a cat, but it was much faster and almost snake-like in its movements. It appeared to flow over the rocks and branches and through the vegetation like liquid: it was a mink.

The speed with which the mink progressed along the bank was startling, yet it missed nothing. Every nook and cranny in the bankside was inspected and every patch of grass or bracken scrutinized in its search for something to eat. Mink are voracious predators, and this was a large one, almost certainly a male. Its coat was a shiny black, unlike the dark brown of the otter, for which it is sometimes mistaken.

The dipper nest would not stand a chance against this predator, nor would the parents, for that matter, if they were unlucky enough to get caught defending their home. The mink was so engrossed with its search for food that it failed to notice me until it was directly opposite me. Even then, it would have passed without seeing me and carried onwards towards the young dippers. I simply stood up from where I lay hidden in the long grass. The predator turned, gave a startled *thsssp* sound and disappeared into the undergrowth.

It was early in the morning when the young dippers finally left the safety of their nest and ventured out onto the riverside, their incessant calling greeting me as I approached the bridge. The newly fledged birds were sitting on the rocks near its base. There were four of them, and they were sitting in two groups, with two birds in each. Their proximity to the bridge suggested they may only have left the nest shortly before my arrival.

The young dippers were strange-looking birds, barely resembling their parents at all. Not only was their plumage utterly different, their overall shape and proportions were distinctly at odds with those of the adults. Their upper parts were a dark steel-grey with pale barring, while their pale underparts were densely marked with grey, wavy lines. Unlike the adults' extensive white bibs, the youngsters only showed small, restricted white throat-patches.

Although they appeared the same size as the adults, they lacked their chunky, dumpy and short-legged aspect. Instead, they looked slim and unusually long-legged. They also held their tails raised most of the time, unlike the adults, which only cocked theirs occasionally. To my eyes they looked very like an unusual type of thrush. They would retain this odd plumage for several months, before moulting into their adult colours.

The young birds remain dependent on their parents for many weeks after they leave the nest. By the end of that first day, the family had split up and moved away from the bridge. Each parent, whether intentionally or not, had taken responsibility for two offspring each. The two siblings of a given group would perch alongside each other at the edge of the bank, while the parent responsible for them endlessly foraged nearby, bringing food every couple of minutes to each chick in turn.

During the subsequent days and weeks, the fledglings clamoured for food from dawn until dusk. Their incessant calling became a familiar backdrop as I made my way along the riverbank. Having left the nest, they were in no hurry to gain further independence, and their parents continued to feed them well into the summer.

Months later, even once they had acquired the ability to feed themselves, I often saw them feeding alongside their parents. Sometimes they would still adopt the begging posture of a newly fledged youngster, crouching down with their fluttering wings held out from their bodies, all the time calling loudly. But by this stage their pleas would no longer be answered, and the parents simply ignored them.

While the young dippers were in the process of leaving their nest, and as I continued looking for the kingfisher, the solitary woodpecker continued its lonely vigil under my ever-watchful gaze. The eggs of the great spotted woodpecker take about twelve days to hatch once incubation has started. Because I did not know the date the final egg in the clutch had been laid, it was not possible for me to accurately predict the day the eggs would hatch.


DURING THE WEEK that followed my discovery of the eggs, I passed many an hour keeping the single-parent family under scrutiny. For most of the time there was little to be seen, as the male sat for long periods inside the tree, far longer than during my previous nest observations. But then, none of my previous observations had involved just one bird tackling such a formidable task alone. We were both in unknown territory.

The pattern of his efforts remained much the same throughout our shared vigil. He would sit on the eggs for several hours before emerging for as brief a feeding excursion as possible. But then, as we approached the end of the second week, he became far more active and began to emerge every ten or fifteen minutes. As I watched him return, he landed at the nest hole and paused before going inside. Looking closely, I could just make out that he was carrying food in his bill. The eggs had hatched.

Once again, we arrived in the clearing with our ropes, ladders and cameras. Securing the ladder to the tree, my friend scaled the trunk to just below the hole, with me nervously climbing as far as the fourth rung. 'How are you getting on?' I shouted helpfully.

'Shh, hear that?' came an instruction from above. I strained to listen from below, and sure enough I heard a low purring sound: the cries of young woodpecker chicks.

Inserting the flexible optical cable through the entrance hole, we switched on the camera. As before, fissured and rotten wood swam into view. Twisting and turning the camera in a desperate effort to get it looking in the right direction just produced a series of images of the inside of the tree. Finally, a new image filled the screen: a pale, misshapen mass lay at the bottom of the chamber.

The newly hatched chicks were blind and naked, which is normal for all newly hatched woodpecker chicks. With no feathers to trap their body heat, they huddled together for warmth. Although the chicks were only a day or two old, dark feather sheaths were already visible, mainly along their backs and stubby wings, from which their actual feathers would soon emerge. They made a strange sight, as their bills looked out of proportion to their bodies, being longer than those of any other newborn chicks I had seen.

I could not tell how many were in the nest, since they were piled together in a heap. I counted four bills protruding from the edges of the group, but it was likely that other chicks were hidden from view under their topmost siblings. With their long beaks and bare, stubby 'arms', they looked like baby pterosaurs – those leathery-winged flying reptiles from eras long past – rather than one of our most charismatic woodland birds.

Now that the young woodpeckers had hatched, the male stepped up his activity considerably. He was active from first light until about an hour before dusk, which in mid-May is a considerable portion of the day. With two parents in attendance, an adult would normally return to the nest about once every ten to fifteen minutes. Often they alternate visits so that each parent makes about three to four trips per hour to feed the chicks. With four to six chicks in the nest, clearly this would not be successful in the present situation, as some of the weaker chicks might only get fed once every ninety minutes. This was too long an interval to sustain so many fast-developing bodies.

However, their father seemed to understand his children's needs, and from dawn to dusk he operated at a speed that was impressive beyond belief. Sometimes he foraged in the trees alongside the nest or in the leaf litter on the woodland floor below. By doing so, he was able to bring food to the nest as frequently as every couple of minutes. This enabled him to make forays further afield once the chicks' appetites had been sated, either to feed himself or to exploit a rich food resource not available in the immediate vicinity of the nest.

One such food resource was the oil- and protein-rich peanuts provided in a feeder in a garden across the river, at the edge of the woods. This garden had a long history of visitations by the woodpeckers from the Spanish chestnut. The feeder was located almost half a kilometre away, so a journey of almost a kilometre was required for each beakful of food brought back to the nest. In preceding years, both parents would generally arrive at the feeder during their chicks' final week in the nest.

There is an enormous growth spurt during that final week, and, since the chicks are by then fully feathered, they can survive longer gaps between feeds. But this year the male began visiting the garden feeder by the end of the first week: he had made an executive decision that the extra time away from the nest would be offset by the high energy value of the peanuts.

I thought it was a risky strategy; the chicks were not being brooded for warmth, and there was no parent to guard the nest. It would be interesting to see whether his strategy would work.

The owners of the garden had enjoyed the exploits of the woodpeckers for many years, since the parents usually brought the chicks to the feeder about a week after they had left the nest. In the weeks leading up to this event, the woodpeckers' visits to the feeder usually lasted for about five minutes. The bird would first feed itself, then load up its bill with food before beginning the return journey to the nest. This year, however, was not the relaxed affair of previous years.

The male was described by the owners as 'run ragged' or 'frazzled'. He would arrive and frantically cram as many peanuts into his bill as possible, before flying off on a direct vector towards the nest. His visits lasted only a minute, sometimes less. Watching from my hide, I would see him arriving over the treetops from across the river. His bounding flight took him not into the canopy of a nearby tree, from where he would have scanned the area for predators before flying to the nest hole. No, his flight path took him directly to the entrance of the nest, where he would instantly vanish from view. When he re-emerged moments later, having fed the chicks, he would once again bound across treetops in the direction of the never-ending supply of peanuts.

THE DAYS PASSED, and the chicks continued to grow. Their calls gradually evolved from the purring sounds of the first few days through a series of distinct vocalization changes. This enabled me to identify their stages of growth, then apply this knowledge to other woodpecker nests in the area, nests whose egg-laying date or hatching date I had yet to ascertain. By the end of the first week, the sounds had moved from a gentle *purrrrrr ... purrrrrr ... purrrrrr* to a *kee-kee-kee-kee-kee-kee*.

By the second week, this in turn had strengthened to a *keek-keek-keek*. By the end of the third week, their cries would be almost inseparable from those of the adult, consisting of a single, sharp, characteristic *kik* note. Almost inseparable, but not quite. For about a month after they leave the nest, I find the call note of the youngsters to be identifiable, although many other naturalists and birdwatchers are unable to pick out the subtle differences in intonation. To my ears, the call of the young birds after they have left the nest and gained their independence is ever so slightly softer and hesitant than those made by the adults; it is almost as though the juveniles, as yet, lack the confidence to be heard.

And it was not just their calls that changed over the hours, days and weeks I watched them – their behaviour changed too as they developed inside the tree. The floor of the nesting chamber is located about twenty centimetres below the entrance hole. When the chicks are only a few days old, the parent bird has to go completely inside the tree to feed them before coming back out again.

As the chicks grow and become stronger, they start to climb the inner walls of the tree to meet the parents on their return. By the middle of the second week, the parent bird only needs to press its head and shoulders inside the nest hole to feed the youngsters, which are clinging to the inside of the nest like a group of mountaineers scaling a cliff face. From this stage on, less and less time is spent by the parent birds inside the nest.

They will go inside on every second or third visit to remove a faecal sack, containing the waste products produced by one of the chicks. Woodpeckers are scrupulous housekeepers, and they keep the inside of the nest almost pristine. Examination of nests after the chicks have flown shows a clean base to the nesting chamber: clear proof of the parents' diligence.

Eventually the chicks' continuing development brings them to the stage where they sit at the entrance hole, peering out at the world outside their nest. Most young great spotted woodpeckers have a red crown, unlike the black crowns of the adult birds. The extent of red on each chick varies, sometimes quite considerably: some youngsters have a lot of red, others less and occasionally none at all. Taking turns, the chicks often sit for prolonged periods at the entrance hole, calling *kik-kik-kik*.

I have always been intrigued by how noisy woodpecker chicks are in the nest. It seems a contradiction to a survival strategy developed over millennia. The birds spend considerable efforts excavating a safe refuge deep within a tree, yet the chicks call continuously for their parents' attention, and with such vivacity and high-spiritedness that they can be heard several metres away from the nest. If I could hear them, then so could a predator. Although they were located inside a tree, that did not guarantee their safety from a pine marten.

Without question, the pine marten is my favourite native Irish mammal. They are sleek, elegant and sinuous, beautiful to look at, with a luscious coat and a tail so furry and bushy that it seems to float in the air behind them. However, from a woodpecker's perspective, they are a shrewd, sharp-toothed and razor-clawed package of death. In recent years, pine martens have increased in numbers and have started to add great spotted woodpecker chicks to their varied diet. When they locate a nest, invariably when the chicks are at their noisiest, they scale the tree and, using their claws and teeth, they rip out the wood from below the nest entrance or, more typically, from the back of the tree. Rarely, for whatever reason, do they gain access through the entrance hole itself.

I have often felt that unless the woodpeckers learn to contain their youngsters' exuberance in calling, they are doomed to failure. With every passing year, ever more woodpecker nests fall prey to this woodland hunter in County Wicklow. There is no half-measure with a pine marten attack either: all chicks will be killed and the nest rendered unusable for future seasons. Despite many nests succumbing to predation, the nest in my Spanish chestnut tree has escaped notice from these sharp-eyed mustelids since first being used in 2011. This is quite amazing, as pine martens are resident in this woodland, and I have both seen and photographed them a short distance from the tree itself.

The chicks continued to develop under the continuing care and attention lavished on them by their father. We made one more foray up to the nest with the camera towards the end of the second week. Once again, we struggled to get the camera into the right position, but we were eventually rewarded with a lovely close-up of well-developed chicks. They were now fully feathered, looking more like woodpeckers than baby dinosaurs. I counted at least three chicks, and the suggestion of a fourth.

The bottom of the nesting cavity looked to be full of chicks, and if there were five or six it would have been impossible to see them all. Unusually, due to their cramped surroundings, woodpecker chicks do not sit in a single layer as do most other birds, such as robins or blackbirds. Inside the tree, they make a pyramid, with the most recently fed chicks at the bottom. The hungriest chicks sit at the pinnacle of the pyramid, and so get fed first. Only when they are fully fed do they change places with those at the bottom of the pile.

It was now the third week since hatching, and the male woodpecker had done an astounding job of single-handedly getting the chicks to this stage in their development. Who could fail to be impressed by his commitment, his dedication and his determination to succeed? I had never seen such a loving father – nor one that looked as shattered as he did!

Great spotted woodpeckers normally take their maiden flight twenty-three to twenty-six days after hatching. Over the years, I have been fortunate to witness this leap of faith – this jump into the unknown – on several occasions. I have watched, like a proud parent, with a lump in my throat as they have spread their wings and left the only world they have known. Crossing a threshold, they ventured into a realm beyond anything their young minds could have envisioned. No matter how many times I saw it I never tired of it, and this year was no different.

When I approached the nest on day twenty-two, my arrival was, as always, greeted by a chorus of *kik-kik* calls from the almost full-grown chicks. Suddenly, the smile on my face and my conviction that all was well crumbled and collapsed as I stared at a series of four parallel lines on the trunk of the tree. My heart started to beat loudly in my chest, filling my ears with its pulse.

Pine marten claw marks!

The more I examined the tree, the more marks I found. The soft wood of the slowly decaying tree had offered little resistance, and the gouges from the marten's claws were clearly visible, not just in the bark at the bottom of the tree, but higher up towards the nest hole as well. I was certain that they had not been there on my previous visit, yet the young had not been taken. This was surprising, as I had no doubt that the tree was an easy one for a pine marten to burrow into ... perhaps my arrival had disturbed it?

Like other animals in this woodland, pine martens also have families at this time of year. Usually this species is predominantly nocturnal or at the very least crepuscular, meaning they are also active at twilight. However, with up to four hungry young kits to feed, the mother marten often ventures out during the daytime, especially in quiet woods such as this. I knew if I left things as they were, the chicks would likely be killed before the following morning. They were only a day or so from succeeding – intervention was needed if I wanted my family to live!

I quickly made a few phone calls from my woodland hide, all the time watching out for the marten's return. Within an hour, a friend arrived in his jeep with a large, coiled sheet of aluminium, about two metres in height and three metres in length. With a small amount of difficulty, we managed to get this sheet onto the trunk of the Spanish chestnut, securing it with several heavy-duty screws. By the time we had finished, we had created a large metal sleeve extending from the woodland floor up the tree.

The smooth, unyielding surface of the metal offered no grip or foothold to the pine marten, thus hopefully preventing it from getting to the woodpecker chicks. As always, I waited after my friend departed to ensure all was well before leaving myself. Within minutes the chicks were leaning out of the nest hole calling *kik-kik* as their father approached carrying food. All was indeed well.

As I made my way to the nest the following morning, my mind was lurching from argument to argument inside my head. They'll be killed, I should have stayed ... They'll be fine, nothing can climb up metal ... What if the pine marten is there now? ... Do I intervene? ... This is nature, accept it!

My arrival at the woodland glade was greeted with silence. No *kik-kik* calls emanated from the tree, or from anywhere else in the woodland. My heart sank once again. I rapidly made my way to the tree. There was no sign of predation anywhere on the trunk, and no fresh claw marks could be detected on the bark above the metal sheet. Had the chicks really flown on day twenty-two or twenty-three? More importantly, had they really flown without my supervision?

Watching from my hide provided neither further information nor further sightings, nor did a walk through the surrounding woods, where I was only met with an expanding vacuum of woodpecker activity. But although my direct observations on the nest had now ceased for another year, the story itself never ceases, it merely develops.

It was not long before I received a phone call to say that a male woodpecker, accompanied by at least three juveniles, had arrived at the peanut feeder in the garden beside the woodland. According to the owners, this was the earliest date ever for a family to arrive.

Reviewing the events around that family in my head later that night, I constructed a scenario. Although woodpecker chicks are well developed by the twenty-second day after hatching, here in Ireland they usually remain in the nest for another few days. I think that the valiant efforts of the male provided enough food for the young to grow and develop, but not enough to be complacent about leaving.

As soon as they were able, at twenty-two days old, they jumped ship, so to speak. Although well fed, they were probably still sufficiently hungry to be driven from the security of their nest slightly earlier than normal. Their father, probably exhausted from his five-week struggle, then immediately led them straight to the richest food source he knew – peanuts.

I always enjoyed seeing the woodpecker family after they left the nest, and this year was no different. I made my way to the garden and watched from the shelter of an old apple tree. Even though it was now early summer, the peanut feeders in the garden were far from devoid of birdlife. Great tits and coal tits were the most regular visitors to this bonanza of free food, interspersed with chaffinches, robins and even the occasional siskin.

Watching the frantic flurry of wings, my eye caught a movement near the top of a silver birch, and I spotted the distinctive silhouette of a great spotted woodpecker. As I watched, other woodpecker outlines became apparent in the surrounding tree canopies. I counted four birds, but there could have been more hidden amongst the foliage. One bird glided down onto a feeder, not more than fifteen metres from where I sat, sending the other, smaller birds scattering in fright.

Its bright-red crown instantly identified it as a juvenile. Then another bird glided down to join the youngster – the male. The two of them sat on the feeders, the male watching cautiously around while his offspring fed enthusiastically. It was a lovely family portrait, and its significance was not wasted on me. This single bird had managed to raise a family against all the odds. Alone, with no possibility of sharing any of the duties, he had managed to incubate, hatch and rear most, if not all, of his six offspring, which I had seen for the first time as eggs more than five weeks earlier. How he had kept it all together amazed me, and yet it was still not the end of the story.

He would continue to look after his young charges for a further two to three weeks, protecting them and teaching them to survive in what, for them, was often a perilous environment. But that lay in the future, and for now all was peaceful as he hung onto the bottom of the feeder, his eyes half-closed in the early summer sun. I smiled to myself at the serenity of the scene before me, and as the proud father turned his head to look in my direction ... I imagined he was smiling as well.

Compared to the ease with which I had studied the woodpeckers over the years, the kingfishers were incredibly hard work. However, during the time in which that lone male great spotted woodpecker hatched the eggs and started to rear his family, I had finally identified a nexus of kingfisher action. On several occasions, on my approach, I had seen a kingfisher fly off from a large branch extending out from a heavily overgrown bank. There was no exposed bank face that I could see, but I felt sure that the area warranted more intense scrutiny.

IT WAS LATE April and still dark when I arose. Sunrise was a long way off, but I wanted to explore that hub of activity I had previously identified as early in the day as possible. Birds are normally quite active at dawn – or even pre-dawn – and their behaviour at that time of day often differs from that of later on.

Despite the darkness that surrounded me when I awoke, it was not long before a paleness stretched across the eastern horizon. It rapidly became suffused with colour, which changed in shade and intensity with every passing minute as the day's eye pushed closer to the still-dark horizon. The stars were gradually being erased from a solitary darkness to be replaced by a cordially welcoming sun. It was a routine, almost mundane, event that happened every day, yet it always made me pause, and hopefully always will.

As I made my way along the river, the first shaft from the glowing disk slipped over the land, illuminating it with low, oblique beams as though it were a stage set. Dew-drenched spiderwebs exploded into existence, each gossamer, veil-like construction glistening as though bedecked with a thousand diamonds. The very feeling of being alive that morning overwhelmed me.

As I approached that central activity point on the river, I looked ahead with my binoculars and saw a kingfisher sitting on the branch. Turning its head, it saw me and took off, and was quickly lost to view. I settled against the large bole of an oak tree and, opening my rucksack, took out a folded, navy bedsheet. When watching the woodpeckers, I had constructed a semi-permanent wooden observation hide, but a 'hide' is nothing more than a screen to prevent a bird, or animal, from recognizing the human shape or form.

I quickly placed the sheet over my head and let it hang loosely down over my body, transforming me into an ill-defined mound, which hopefully any passing kingfisher would ignore. Once I was comfortably seated, I took out a pair of scissors and cut a horizontal slit in the sheet at the same level as my eyes. Looking through this, I was able to scan the river in both directions for any signs of the kingfishers. The advantage of a simple sheet covering, as opposed to a more elaborate fixed structure, was the mobility it offered.

I could change my position on the bank at any time if a more suitable vantage point became evident. A sheet was so versatile, easily transportable and, as well as preventing the birds from seeing me, it kept the hordes of biting midges, predominantly *Culicoides impunctatus*, at bay: with bites out of proportion to their size, these tiny nippers are not to be underestimated.

The biting midges in the Wicklow Mountains belong to the same species as those found in the Scottish Highlands. It may well be unintentional, but they can make wildlife-watching a sheer misery, especially at dawn and dusk, since direct sunlight inhibits them. Within moments of sitting down in any woodland or waterside setting, the familiar biting and subsequent itching – ferocious in its intensity – commences. But the simple act of draping a bedsheet over my body protected me from them, as well as shielding me from the kingfishers' gaze.

About five minutes after I had settled down, a kingfisher flew back to the branch – it was the male. He sat there agitatedly, bobbing up and down, and stretched his neck out so that he went from being small and squat to thin and elongated. After a few minutes of this nervous-energy activity, he flew off once more. I heard him calling after he left, the sound travelling back from further downstream, where he had ventured. Then, he was back – or so I thought.

The glint of pale pink at the base of its bill revealed that it was actually now the female sitting on the branch. Her behaviour was far more unobtrusive than that of her mate. She sat there, motionless for the most part, with none of the male's agitation. Occasionally she looked around, giving a small bob of her head as she did so. A loud whistle, another blaze of blue, and the male landed alongside her, adopting a proud stance like a soldier standing to attention, with his gleaming, black bill pointed skyward.

Full of enthusiasm, he jibbed and jived along the branch, giving short, whistling calls – *peep-peep-peep* – as he did so. The female became very solicitous and adopted a begging position, with her neck craned backwards, her wings slightly fanned and her bill partly opened. I was sure this behaviour was a prelude to mating and expected the male to perform his duties there and then, but that was not to be. He continued to prance along the branch, but she lost interest and began preening her wing feathers.

This part of the river was heavily wooded and overgrown, its banks covered in ferns, brambles and dense undergrowth: I failed to see its hold on the kingfishers' attention. The sun, still low in the early-morning sky, had not extended its reach to the river, and the birds were still in a gloomy, half-lit world of dark water and vegetation. Watching them in this woodland setting was a strange experience – they looked and appeared more like woodland birds than fluvial ones.

Strangely, their colouration somehow blended in with the background, the mosaic of shades and colours breaking up their outlines. The orange underparts become like another russet patch of leaves, while the hints of azure could almost be just a reflected shaft of light. One of our most vibrantly coloured native species, yet it simply melted into the greenery behind – no wonder so many sightings are just of birds flying away.

Watching the pair, undisturbed and at such close quarters, allowed me to examine their plumage in detail. Although identical in markings, the female was distinctly duller in appearance when seen alongside the male. The blue on her crown was less vibrant, and the black spotting within the blue was less defined. The white patches on either side of her neck were less noticeable and lacked the purity of those sported by the male. Even in the shade, with no sunlight to ignite its iridescence, the male's blue feathering sparkled.

Seen from behind, as he turned around on the branch, the azure on his back extended in an unbroken, blazing streak of light from his crown to his tail. The male continued to posture with the female, but there were no advancements towards mating. The male started to make short sorties out from the branch and back again. Each time he flew, he would hover in front of a patch of brambles, like a giant hawkmoth scanning the leaves, before returning to his perch.

This strange behaviour continued: clearly, he was looking for something, but what? The female faced in the other direction, showing no interest in whatever was occupying his attention. Although he wavered along a stretch of riverbank several metres in length, he kept returning to a patch of bramble growing downwards from the bank, forming a tangled and impenetrable screen. All I could see of the shrouded bankside behind were a few small ferns growing slightly above water level.

Again, the male hovered in front of this jungle of growth, then suddenly surprised me by dipping down under the curtain of briars to emerge in front of the ferns. It was as though he had slipped behind a waterfall and entered a hidden world beyond. I could see him, hovering, half-hidden from view, presenting himself only as a hazy, shadowy, almost spiritual form. He approached the ferns and, closing his wings, disappeared.

Moments later, he was back out hovering in front of the veiling vegetation, whistling loudly before flying off to join his disinterested mate. I stared hard at the fern-covered patch of bank through my binoculars, trying to ignore the haze created by the out-of-focus vegetation in the foreground. There, just below the largest fern, partly shielded by the overhanging fronds, was a dark, circular-shaped shadow: an entrance hole.

Once more the male left the female and hung hovering in the air in front of the leafy screen, before dropping down under it and pausing mid-flight in front of the nest entrance. Then he dropped into the burrow, clinging to the floor of the tunnel with his small, blood-red feet, still flapping his wings to steady himself against the bank. Folding his wings, he shuffled into the darkness within. This time he did not return as promptly as before. I sat there watching the female on the riverside for almost ten minutes before he whistled his departure from their riverbank nest and rejoined her. What had he been doing in there, I wondered?

Finally finding this nest had been a great achievement and, given the hours of fieldwork involved, represented possibly the hardest nesting site I have ever tried to locate. Some secretive species, such as warblers or larks, have very well-hidden nests, but their territories are easy to identify. It is relatively straightforward to follow their lifestyle and habits during the breeding season, even without locating the nest. However, it had taken me two months merely to identify the approximate boundaries of the territory of this pair of kingfishers.

The location and siting of this nest was educational for me, to say the least; in fact, it was the complete antithesis to everything I thought I knew about kingfisher nests. All the banks I had surveyed as being potentially suitable were exposed, bare and open-faced sites. Easy to excavate, and with a clear, direct line of approach to the nest, had been my expectation of the pair's key requirements.

This nest burrow, however, was so well hidden amongst vegetation that it may as well have been invisible. In fact, there was little exposed soil on this bank into which a bird could tunnel at all. It was possible that there had been another fern growing there on the bank, which had died and fallen off, exposing a patch of clay, which the kingfishers could then tunnel into. The small section of tunnel entrance that was visible did not seem recently excavated, and I suspected that this nest site may have been used in previous years.

The male did not seem to have been excavating while he was inside the burrow, and with both birds sitting outside the nest it was unlikely that incubation was underway. Again, the question remained: why had he been sitting deep inside the bank for almost ten minutes? I was still occupied by this thought when the female abruptly flew from the branch to the nest. Without any hovering or procrastination, she flew straight under the brambles and up into the nest hole; in an instant, she was gone. The male sat there for another minute or so before flying upstream, his accompanying shrill whistling bounding off the riverbanks as he flew.

I waited for half an hour, but neither bird put in any further appearance. The echo of that whistle had faded away to nothing, and just the sound of the river remained. The endlessly changing murmuring, rippling, tinkling and laughing sounds of the water infused the surrounding woodland with a lively backdrop of sound. It was a relaxing place, a rejuvenating place: an ideal place for a spirit to reside ...

A perfect place for both the kingfishers and myself to spend the coming months.

# GATHERING STORM

NOW THAT THE nesting site had been identified, I was finally able to focus my attention on watching rather than searching for kingfishers. Depending on the time I had available, the duration of my observations and the time of day during which they were carried out varied from one day to the next. Sometimes when I arrived there would be no sign of either bird, and it would take a while for me to discover where they were and what they were up to.

One of the pair often sat inside the burrow for lengthy periods of time, but that did not necessarily mean it was sitting on eggs. I have watched woodpeckers sitting inside the nest hole for hours in early April, yet the eggs are often not laid until late April. Kingfishers are no different in this respect, and I had sometimes seen the birds fly into the nest only to leave it an hour later, not returning for a long while. In such cases, they are clearly not incubating, but without prolonged observation it would be impossible to know this.

After my previous successful sunrise visit, which had helped me to locate the nest, I decided to channel more of my efforts into this time of the day. Although I love the rewards that an early-morning reverie brings, I often fail to embrace enough of them. The off-switch in my mind simply does not work quite the way it does with others. I often have difficulty sleeping and, when deprived of slumber, rarely embrace the dawn with relish.

Thankfully, sunrise at this time of year was not offputtingly early; it was unnecessary to embark before 4.30 am. But that first sight of the sky when I stepped through the door, that revelation, made me wish I had scheduled each day of my life to commence with this event ...

The darkness behind me was still complete and extended above me, before gradually retreating as it approached the eastern boundary – and what a boundary! The sun's disk was still well below the horizon, and the world seemed frozen in anticipation. The canvas it was creating was as red as a poppy and torn with jagged, gold lightning, before bleeding into velvet blue and disappearing into the colour of infinity. A thin river of gold, formed by the edges of clouds on the horizon, extended from the darkness and across the growing tapestry: it lay there, like an old-fashioned explosive fuse. And then it exploded.

The most imperceptible of arc-shaped lines erupted from the ground and grew at an astonishing rate. Like a kingfisher emerging from a dive, being reborn from the life-giving water, the glowing phoenix arose from the ashes of the darkness and the day erupted across the landscape. Colour flooded my eyes as I beheld the dawn, seeing something never before witnessed, something no other living person had seen – a moment, fresh and unique, that belonged to me and no one else. And with that silent explosion came sound, sound which was prompted by the explosion, yet not generated by it: birdsong.

Now, in early summer, the choral troupe had reached its maximum. Robins, song thrushes, blackbirds, dunnocks, wrens, blue tits, great tits, chaffinches and the first swallows, recently arrived from South Africa. The swallows were not the only visitors from Africa to partake in the performance. A host of warblers had arrived: blackcaps, chiffchaffs, willow warblers and whitethroats all contributed with a variety of lively, musical songs. And, distantly, a cuckoo announced its presence with its name.

The chorus was amazing, overwhelming, an ensemble performance that seemed to have erupted spontaneously, but I knew it could not have. The birds had undoubtedly been singing as I was waiting for the sun to creep above the horizon, but I was so absorbed and distracted by the colourful spectacle that I had been deaf to my surroundings. Overhead came yet another sound, beautifully evocative yet an intrusion into the chorus; it was a solo recital, not a chorale. The bird called as it wheeled over my head, *wheeeeoooooo,* before banking sharply to its right and disappearing behind the regimental ranks of sitka spruce that covered this part of the hillside I was standing on. Larger than the buzzard, this bird commandeered attention and dominated the skies in which it lived, due to its size, grace and dignity. The red kite, without doubt the king of the birds here in the Wicklow Mountains, was a master of the winds and currents that circled the hills around me.

Long, angular wings carried this bird on a patchwork of thermals and airstreams, over woods, along valleys and across lakes. With barely a flap, it soared over distances in the blink of an eye, feeling each fluctuation in air pressure and adjusting its wings accordingly. Its broad, forked tail turned and twisted constantly and often frantically, like a person with a sailboard desperately trying to catch the light sea breezes of a summer's day.

MANY OF THE birds and animals I watch in Wicklow have interesting stories to tell about how they came to live here. The great spotted woodpecker colonized the area in the early 2000s from Britain, flying across the Irish Sea as part of a European population explosion. The kingfisher, on the other hand, has always been here, since the glaciers last retreated to their northern refuges. The pine marten has also dwelt here since the last ice age. However, extermination by mankind drove it out of Wicklow, and much of the island, to lands west of the River Shannon. Like the woodpeckers, it returned in the early 2000s, although, unlike the woodpeckers, it was recolonizing formerly held territory.

The red kite also has a story to tell of its arrival here in Wicklow, a story which differs considerably from those of the others. It belongs to a group of birds called raptors, sometimes dubbed 'birds of prey'. These include small species such as the kestrel and sparrowhawk, as well as much larger ones such as the eagle. Although red kites are one of Ireland's largest raptors, they are still significantly smaller than eagles.

Formerly a native breeding species, they were exterminated due to human persecution, and their cries ceased to be heard in these valleys over two hundred years ago. The presence of the bird overhead was the result of a very successful reintroduction programme conducted over many years. While a welcome sight in our skies, I never feel the same enthusiasm for reintroduced species as I do for those, such as the great spotted woodpecker, who colonized unaided by humankind.

AS I ARRIVED at the river and began walking along the bank towards the kingfishers' nest site, the male grey wagtail spotted me and began calling. His shrill, ringing *tzeet-tzeet-tze-tseet* notes carried easily in the chilly morning air. His family were roughly half-grown at this stage, and the almost insatiable appetite of those four mouths would keep both him and his mate busy for many days yet.

A short distance further on, I encountered some of the dipper family: two chicks and an attendant adult, most likely the male, judging by the width of the chestnut breast-band. The two youngsters were frantically calling *pee-pee-pee-pee-pee-peeeeee-pee-pee-pee-pee-pee-peeeeee* as they furiously flapped their wings while balancing precariously upon a rock. As always, the male was unmoved by their hysterical pleas and foraged neither faster, nor with any additional urgency, than if he were just feeding himself.

Torn between wanting to stay and keen to push on towards my goal, I reluctantly left the dippers, although their frenzied calls followed me for quite some distance. I was still enthralled at how overwhelmingly fantastic a day it was, and the lure of the kingfishers' nest struggled against my urge to just sit and enjoy. There was colour and sound everywhere that morning, as well as a spectrum of stimuli for the other senses: scents, flavours and textures. Nature influences our well-being, both mentally and physically, in ways we often barely perceive. Yet so many of us fail to harness or embrace its power – a cure offered to us free, and with no consultation required.

The sensory stimulation provided by nature has been employed to great effect in the vogueish development of sensory gardens, primarily aimed at children faced with challenges in understanding the world around them. Wind sighs through drifts of tall grasses and creaks its way amongst stands of bamboo. The scents of sweet pea, honeysuckle and rose sail through drifts of brightly coloured blooms set amongst furry and sticky-leaved, ground-covering plants.

But all of this wealth, this treasure, can be found wherever nature is allowed her freedom to create, and, upon being found, can provide opportunities to set our minds free. And today her creation was in evidence all around me as I ran my hand along the bole of an ancient willow beside me. The rough, fissured bark on the trunk was in sharp contrast to the velvety softness of the moss that partially covered it. Interspersed amongst the mosses were lichens, the crusty feel of which added a final layer of texture to this ageing sentinel. Swirls of warm coconut scent emanated from the nearby gorse bushes. Overhead, the mewling cry of a buzzard floated downwards from a blue sky, dotted with popcorn-shaped, puffy clouds. And behind it all, the rippling, crooning sounds of the river, which laughed its way through the woodland on its ceaseless journey.

As I pulled myself away from this indulgence – or necessity, depending on your viewpoint – something long, slender and white caught my eye on the surface of the water along the opposite bank. Refocusing my attention, I realized the body of a grey heron was floating there. Fortunately, I was not too far from a bridge and I was able to cross the river, and within a short time I had reached the bank where the bird's body lay.

I knew straight away it was an adult bird by its bright-orange, dagger-shaped bill and clearly defined black crown and forehead. The body had likely been washed downstream and come to rest here, away from the main flow of the river. The water lapped against the riverbank, causing the heron's body to bump and rock against the stones. I reached in and gently lifted it from the water, my arms supporting its body and neck as its lifeless head dangled downwards, its bill and its feet trailing in the water.

The sight of the dead bird in my arms affected me, it disturbed me … something, from somewhere, had intruded into my day.

Having spent my life surrounded by animals, both pets and those living in the wild, the death of an animal was nothing new. Nor was the sadness I always felt when looking at a perfectly formed body, a frame which only lacked that unquantifiable spark of life. It was probably a difficult tightrope for my parents and siblings to walk – the more pets and animals they helped me surround myself with, the more days of distress and consolation they would have to engage in.

Cats, gerbils, budgies, terrapins, sparrows, frogs – even poor Fred the herring gull – all left a trail of sadness with their passing, despite all the happiness they had imparted to me in life. The pet cemetery in the garden began to grow at an extraordinary rate with each passing year. Every flower bed had a resident or two entombed in the soil, usually wrapped in a cloth to stop the soil from dirtying them.

Looking at the heron's beautifully marked plumage, I followed the India ink-like markings painted along its snow-white neck. A series of dots and dashes, a Morse code uninterpretable by humankind, a language confined to herons and meaningless except in its beauty. My mind began to travel. I had seen this type of pattern before … and held it in my hands as well. And it wasn't a happy memory.

THE SPOTS HAD belonged to another Dalmatian, a companion like no other, with whom I had shared my previous ramblings, several years ago. Like her successor (who was patiently awaiting my return home), she too had explored the countryside with me. The two of us, a team, had shared a bond far stronger than any I shared with people, both those around me and those closest to me. Together we had explored winter landscapes of mountains, rivers and woodlands, where dark, turbulent waters reflected leaden-coloured skies and the sombre, brooding greenness of the ivy-clad oaks. The ground around us lay littered with rain-flattened bracken and walnut-toned oak leaves as we listened to the loud whistle of a kingfisher, followed by its blaze of royal blue and orange.

We chatted, joked and laughed our way through the woodlands, as together we watched the early stages of colonization by the great spotted woodpeckers. Squashed beside each other inside my small, roughly constructed wooden hide, we watched the woodpeckers feeding and rearing their youngsters. We shared our lunches, or at least she shared mine! Some of the viewing holes in the walls of the hide were at the right level for her to see through and, like me, she would peer out across the glade.

Sitting there in the woods or on the banks of the river, sharing Hobnobs and fig rolls, we would watch the world go by. Her limpid brown eyes communicated her every thought as easily as the constant, quizzical flickering of her eyebrows or the ceaseless wag of her tail. My attachment and dependency on her, so natural to me yet so estranging to others, inadvertently laid the foundations of a wall of disenchantment.

Her death had come as unexpectedly as it had been gradual, and worse, while she was still in her prime. I remembered cradling her head in my hands as she took her last breaths, all the while whispering a constant dialogue into her silky, spotted ears ... of the times we had shared ... the places we had been to ... and the things we had seen. I had no way of knowing if she could still hear me during those final moments, but I told her to wait for me at 'the bridge' and not to cross without me. Did she hear me tell her I would come for her, and the others? Even if she heard me, she probably did not understand my words; but hopefully she recognized the reassuring tone of my voice and knew she wasn't crossing alone.

Her death changed how I viewed the world, and, in a way, it prepared me for the wasteland that lay ahead in an undreamt-of future, venturing over an unknown territory. I realized that no one seemed to share or understand my loss, and to be honest, at the time, that baffled me. I was surrounded by people, yet living in isolation. As a result, I built a wall of disharmony across many, if not all, aspects of my world, as my treasured companion lay buried under a geranium plant, close to where I often sat alone with my early-morning coffee. Even the arrival of a small, white puppy covered in black spots a few weeks later failed entirely to break down that wall, but at least I had a companion with which to explore the surrounding countryside again.

THE COLD RIVER water had, by this stage, dribbled from the heron's saturated plumage along my arms and had begun to soak into my sleeves. The chill gradually extending into my body jolted me out of the past and back to the present. Disharmony and grief were replaced with the practical decision of what to do with the lifeless body I now held. I ran my hands along the bird's breastbone. It was clearly defined, like the keel of a ship, with no layers of subcutaneous fat to soften its lines. To my surprise, the heron was emaciated – it had literally starved to death.

It is not unusual for birds to die of starvation. Harsh weather, like snow, often results in many fatalities amongst our smaller, insect-eating birds such as wrens. Young birds that fail to learn successful hunting techniques often die from starvation also. But neither explanation applied to this poor heron. Firstly, it was an adult bird, at least two years old, which had obviously mastered the skills required to pursue its prey. Secondly, it was spring, and the weather was anything but harsh. Parasites or disease were the remaining options, and I was no expert in either. I placed the heron gently back into the water and left it to continue its journey. With no further distractions, I continued onwards to where the kingfishers' nest was located.

I arrived at my watchpoint, taking care not to make too sudden an approach. Although I saw no kingfisher upon my arrival, I thought I heard one whistling distantly: perhaps, unbeknownst, I had been spotted.

Despite the time of year, there had been quite a noticeable frost. This is not unusual in the Wicklow Mountains, where night-time temperatures often fall several degrees lower than in surrounding areas. Each blade of grass had been coated with a cold, crystalline shroud, a veil so delicate that the warmth of a hand or the first touch of the sun's breath causes it to vanish. As I had walked through the grass, layer upon layer of sparkling, glittering crystals had accumulated on my boots, building up until my feet began to look like paws.

The sun, shining through the tangled web of branches that spanned the river, now projected its rays across the adjacent grass field, while wraiths of rising steam transformed the landscape into a scene in which King Arthur and his knights would not have looked out of place. Each gorse bush that grew alongside the river was draped in countless spiderwebs. Each had caught the night's dew and been transformed into dreamcatchers of every conceivable pattern. What dreams had passed through this landscape last night, I wondered, and whose were they? Only the spiders knew the answer to that. I settled against the bough of the tree, draped the bedsheet over me and melted into the landscape.

The kingfishers' nest lay hidden, both in the undergrowth and the early-morning shade, and attracted no attention from the uninitiated. It was so well hidden that, even though I stared intently, I could not make out the burrow entrance. The irony of this wasn't wasted on me, having seen so many photographs from England over the years of 'typical' nest sites.

There was no bare bank face, no strategic perch, no whitewash below a distinctive burrow ... nothing but undergrowth and brambles. No wonder I had failed to find nests in previous years. I now realized, maybe not for the first time, that very often I did not know what I was looking for, even though I was sure at the time that I did.

A loud, clear whistle refocused my attention, and a kingfisher flew past me, only a few metres from where I sat, heading around the bend further upstream. It had made no attempt to land near the nest. I wondered whether the call had been a greeting to its mate, to let it know that it was still patrolling the territory, or perhaps an alarm signalling the strange object on the bank not too far from the nest site? Or perhaps neither of these, but rather a call uttered simply for the pleasure of hearing it resounding along the riverside?

A few minutes later it reappeared, flying towards me and landing on a branch about a hundred metres away. Fortunately, it was a brightly lit section of the river, and I was able to see the colour of the bill clearly enough to identify it as the male. He sat very alert, with his neck and body stretched upwards, so that he appeared long and slim, rather than his more usual dumpy posture. He was whistling loudly as he agitatedly turned his head from side to side, bobbing it up and down at the same time. Such was his excitement that he was unable to restrain himself.

All of a sudden, his mate alighted alongside, and the pair began a whistling duet. They looked not unlike a pair of swordfish, with their half-opened bills waving around and pointing skyward. Their greeting display over, they settled down and began to preen. The female had most likely spent the past few hours inside the riverbank incubating the eggs, and was now in need of a stretch and a good clean. The male had brought no fish with him, so it appeared that courtship feeding, to strengthen their bond and provide additional nutrition for the female, was no longer required.

There was no urgency about the pair to return to the business of incubation. Although eggs need to be kept warm to hatch, and ideally at a constant temperature, they can remain perfectly viable without a parent sitting on them for quite some time. A lot depends on the species and the nest site.

A wading bird, such as a curlew, has a nest which is highly exposed if the sitting bird departs. This leaves it vulnerable to predators, as well as to the weather. Rain and wind will quickly chill eggs, to the point they become non-viable. Species like this rarely leave their nest unattended, and a bird will usually only vacate its post when its mate returns to relieve it. This strategy applies to all birds whose nests are open to the elements: gulls, terns, waders, ducks and many others.

But my kingfishers, and also my woodpeckers, did not face these challenges. Their nests were less at risk from predators because they were hidden deep inside a bank – or, in the case of the woodpeckers, a tree. Leaving the nest unattended for short periods posed not so great a risk. The chamber in which the eggs lay also had its own a microclimate. With no rain or wind, the air temperature and humidity, both critical to egg development, remained more constant.

Even with a parent's absence, the embryos inside the eggs would continue to grow and develop, provided that the parent returned within a reasonable length of time. And so, there was no urgency compelling the kingfishers who were able to enjoy some quality time together. Eventually their preening ceased, and the two sat quietly on the branch.

Time seemed to slow; the constant whispering sound of the river and its changing kaleidoscope of shapes, patterns and formulations slowly dulled my senses. The sun had warmed the air, and any trace of frost was long gone. Drifts of bluebells formed a misty gauze of blue as they cut meandering swathes through the grassy banks and nearby woodland. The unfurling leaves on the nearby beech trees were a delicate, chartreuse green, my absolute favourite springtime colour. Displayed against this backdrop of ethereal verdancy, these rivers of blue flowed across the woodland floor, dispelling darkness and giving rise to hope.

And then the phone rang.

The sound of the uninvited intrusion shattered the tranquillity of that almost numinous realm. The kingfishers, alerted by the sound, sat up and grew agitated, both birds anxiously looking left, right and left again in an attempt to identify the source. I desperately fumbled beneath my bedsheet, trying to find the phone, trying to put an end to its increasingly annoying and irritating drone. Why had I not put it on silent? Why had I bothered even to *bring* it?

Bags, coats and a tangled sheet thwarted my efforts at a speedy resolution, and the combination of alien sounds and an unexpectedly moving shape was too much for the kingfishers. With a loud whistle, both birds took off and darted around the corner, out of view …

They took with them the magic of that moment we had shared.

I finally located my phone, noticed that the call came from an unrecognized number and, uncharacteristically for me, answered it.

'Good morning, sir, this is the gardaí.' Polite and all as he sounded, I had a strong suspicion that it was going to be anything other than a 'good morning' from this point onwards. He continued with his pleasantries.

'I was wondering if you might be able to drop into us here in the station to go through a few things?'

I ran through the day's schedule in my head: I was quite a distance away from the station ... needed to check a few woodpecker territories ... still had the kingfishers, grey wagtails and dippers to watch ... and, very importantly, had to collect my dog, having left her behind in the house while I watched the kingfishers.

All things considered, I told the garda that I would be able to drop in later that evening.

'I was thinking more like now,' he replied. That totally threw me.

'What's the urgency?' I enquired, but no matter how I presented them, my queries were deflected with vague responses. The police officer wanted to talk to me urgently yet would give no indication as to why. I was equally as vague when it came to explaining why I was not in a position to cooperate; my inner instinct told me that birdwatching and being concerned for my dog were probably not reasons for my absence that they wanted to hear.

I could sense frustration in the garda's voice – not of anger towards me, but of being in a position of having to do something he really wasn't happy about. I tried reassuring him that I was happy to cooperate, and that, unless it was urgent, I would call into the station in the late afternoon.

'That's too late, we need you in here now – this morning,' he replied. We were going nowhere fast, except in circles.

Again, I asked what it was that they were looking for from me.

'I think we need to arrest you,' he responded.

'You *think*?' came my retort.

'Well, actually, we do need to arrest you,' came the exasperated reply. That changed everything: my day, my world – everything.

Over the next few minutes details emerged, albeit brief and sparse. Apparently, they needed to arrest me because of allegations that had been made against me. Strangely, I needed to be arrested, charged and brought before a judge before the allegations could be investigated – but such is the nature of our judicial system, and I was happy to cooperate. I had done nothing wrong, so where was the harm in being arrested?

We agreed a time for me to present myself, admittedly not as promptly as they had hoped – since they still had not explained the apparent urgency – but allowing time enough for me to achieve some of the more important tasks in my day's schedule. And, with an arrangement in place, we each returned to our own respective worlds.

There was certainly no point in waiting for the kingfishers to return, and I was extremely conscious of the fact that both birds were away from their nest, disturbed by our intrusions. I quickly gathered my belongings and hastily retreated further back along the river towards where I had parked the car. I had hoped to observe the grey wagtails' nest, which was close by, but felt that I should completely vacate the area in the vicinity of the nest to ensure the kingfishers' speedy return. I therefore decided to focus on the dippers instead, as they were generally unperturbed by my presence.

The old stone bridge, which spanned the river and had been home to generations of dippers, caught the morning's rays and reflected them from glistening shards of mica embedded within the carved granite blocks. Both adult birds were there with their four youngsters, two with each parent. Weeks had now passed since the young birds had left their nest, yet they were still highly dependent on their parents for food – or at least so it seemed. Both the male and female foraged endlessly in the shallow, turbid waters, their heads held under the flowing torrent as they searched for the insect larvae their youngsters demanded.

Their offspring balanced uncertainly on semi-submerged rocks, slick with sheets of water and mossy carpets. There was no difference in size between them and their parents except for their tails and their wings. These were both still shorter than those of the adults and would remain so for several more weeks. Their plumage remained otherwise unchanged since they had left the nest.

Their upper parts were smoky-grey with a hint of blue, a soft colour which contrasted with the starkness of the adults' black upper parts. Nor had their white bibs developed the pristine quality of the adults' snowy breasts. Row upon row of crescent-shaped markings formed a chainmail pattern that covered their pale chests and broke up their outline. This helped them hide in a world made up of jagged, disturbed shapes and patterns.

The young made no attempt to feed themselves throughout the morning as I watched them. They called endlessly from their rocky perches, their cries so much part of the river's sound as to become indistinguishable from it. They frantically fluttered their wings, craning their necks forward in an effort to encourage their parents to redouble their efforts. But the adults continued to forage at the same speed, unperturbed, flying back to their offspring only when they had bills full of wriggling larvae.

Although in each case there were two chicks clamouring to be fed, each adult would feed just one, then return to gather more food before flying back again. The strongest of the two chicks would invariably get fed again but, eventually, its appetite would be sated, and it would then be the turn of its less dominant sibling to be fed. As far I could see, neither parent made any attempt to provide the chicks equally with food. They simply placed it into whichever mouth was thrust the furthest forward.

Eventually the hunger cries diminished, and the parents started to feed themselves, swallowing the food they caught and slowly moving downstream away from their family. Left to their own devices and with interest in looking for food, the youngsters began to explore the watery world around them. like a group of children let out into a school playground.

Adult dippers do not 'explore'. They remind me of old-fashioned butlers, with their proud demeanour, tuxedoed presentation and often solitary behaviour. But their children are not so easily stereotyped, and as I watched, all four began to investigate their surroundings in quite an uncharacteristic manner – for dippers, at any rate. They hopped onto the bank and began to walk along half-submerged tree trunks. They did not walk with the short steps of the adults; instead, they walked with big, outward-reaching strides, like explorers setting off on a conquest.

The long, spindly toes at the ends of their thick, pink legs, so different from the slate-grey limbs of the adults, grasped the twigs and branches as they climbed in and out of this bankside entanglement. When they walked like this, they did not have the dumpy, rotund appearance of the adults, but became sleek and stealthy.

It was at times like this that they displayed similarities to thrushes – not one of our Irish 'spotted' species, but those from the Far East, which forage in dense forest undergrowth. But those stealthy strides had a more sinister feel to them as well, and as I watched them, I found myself thinking of packs of hunting dinosaurs, such as velociraptors, and why not? Aeons may have separated them, but one may have given rise to the other.

Watching the dippers had temporarily helped me forget the gardaí, who were anxiously awaiting my arrival. But with the young birds now fed and fewer distractions to occupy my thoughts, my mind once again turned to the impending crisis that awaited me. If one of my kingfishers had flown past, I would never even have noticed it – my sight was now turned inwards, to a world lacking any colour or vibrancy; the antithesis of the kingfishers' realm.


I FINALLY ARRIVED at the garda station, five hours after they had contacted me. I rang the bell and waited.

The garda who answered was not the one to whom I had spoken earlier. He was cheerful, which I took to be a good start. 'Can I help you?' he enquired.

I told him my name, adding, 'I believe you are looking for me?'

With a distinctly puzzled expression, he asked, 'And why are we supposed to be looking for you?'

'I've absolutely no idea,' I said, 'but as far as I know, you need to arrest me ... so here I am.'

Silence followed for several seconds, before the garda quietly said, 'In all the years I've worked here, *no one* has ever arrived saying that! Any idea who wants to arrest you, or why?' he continued.

'Well, another garda spoke to me earlier, so he probably has a better idea about what's going on than I do,' I said. 'Perhaps we can ask him?' I added tentatively.

After taking my name along with a few other details and with another perplexed look, the garda closed the door, saying, 'Wait there until I find out what's going on.' So I sat and waited. Other people came and went, made enquiries regarding what was troubling them, and left. I sat, and stayed.

Outside the window of the station was a river on the last few hundred metres of its journey to the sea. Here, this stretch of water was tidal, the sea making its presence felt almost two kilometres upstream from the coast. It was a familiar area, and I remembered coming here as a teenager to watch birds, especially the kingfisher. It was a well-known wintering haunt of kingfishers, which bred further upriver in the Wicklow Mountains. Indeed, the very kingfishers I had been watching that morning were quite likely to have spent some of the previous winter fishing in the nearby harbour and surrounding creeks.

Although widespread throughout Ireland, the kingfisher is one of those species that is very difficult simply to go and watch whenever the mood strikes. Even in the winter months, when they are regularly spotted in harbours and estuaries, they are encountered more often by chance than design. There were only a few locations in Ireland that I could visit and expect to see a kingfisher with little effort, and during the winter this place was one of them. The irony of this was not lost on me, given how I had come to be there.

'Well, looks like you were right,' said a loud voice, rousing me from my daydream.

'Right about what?' I asked.

The garda looked me with a bemused smile. 'We *are* looking for you – well, the other garda is anyway – and we do need to arrest you; but he's been called away, so you're going to have wait until he returns.'

I could see that there was no chance of me returning to the kingfishers that day, so I resigned myself to a wasted afternoon.

'I don't think you're any threat to society,' he said good-humouredly, 'so just sit there and I'll let you know when he arrives.'

Eventually two gardaí came out, both highly apologetic for the delays and the nature of the incident itself.

'Look,' the female garda said, 'these misunderstandings happen all the time, they're nothing to worry about, people are forever misinterpreting situations.'

They went through the allegations that had been put against me and explained that, absurdly, the best way forward was to arrest me, so I could then go before a judge to explain my case. Due to the nature of the allegations, the gardaí themselves were unable to apply discretion or to make a judgement that the claims were false. In this situation they were powerless. Again the younger of the two gardaí reassured me.

'For someone like yourself, this probably all seems quite intimidating,' she said. 'But, honestly, we get this all the time and it just comes down to processing and procedure. We'll have this sorted as quick as we can, and you can be out of here. However,' she added, 'it would have been easier to sort out if you had got here sooner.'

And now the urgency of their calls this morning became clear. While I had been watching the kingfishers and looking after my dog, they had been trying to get me before a sitting of the local district court: but it was Friday, and the last sitting was at 2 pm, two hours beforehand. I stared at them in disbelief as they suggested the best idea was to charge me and then drive me as quickly as possible to the

Central Criminal Court in Dublin, where they could get a judge to hear the case at a special sitting. The alternative was to 'stay' at the station for the weekend until the district court reopened on the Monday. I clearly remember explaining to them that with two children and a dog to care for, 'staying' at the station was not really an option.

I had spent much of the preceding few months tied to the natural world and its rhythms. Removed from people, I had surrounded myself with the sights, sounds, scents and patterns of a world familiar enough to call my own. But I had been summoned from that domain and had travelled unknowingly into another, one whose rules and systems felt entirely alien. Unlike my realm, which was safe, tranquil and unsophisticated, this was fast, noisy and tainted.

In an ironic effort to secure my freedom, the two gardaí quickly arrested and charged me. Such a straightforward task brought a cascade of procedural complications, which they helped me through: medical forms, residency ... the list was confusing and endless. It was now seven hours since I had left the kingfishers, but it might as well have been seven lifetimes ago. Our big worry was that the Dublin Circuit Criminal Court also closed early on Fridays, but they had been notified of our situation and were expecting us.

With the paperwork finally in order, one of the two gardaí told me, 'Go on outside and get yourself into the car.' The other added, 'We're travelling in the garda estate car parked to the left of the main entrance.'

Once outside, no sooner had I opened the door of the car than one of the gardaí shouted across to me, 'Not the passenger door, Declan – you're in the *back*!'

The journey to Dublin was long, and not just on account of heavy traffic. There had been an accident on the motorway and even our blue, flashing lights did little to speed up our journey. Being familiar with the area I lived in, both gardaí were interested to hear about the woodpeckers and kingfishers I had studied over the preceding years. Throughout the frantic drive – a race against deadlines – the conversation swung from birds to allegations and back to birds. 'I've never seen a kingfisher, and I never knew we had woodpeckers in Ireland,' said one of my companions, a comment I had encountered all too often.

Talking about nature helped me relax, and I felt the anxiety, which had been eating away at me for the previous few hours, start to fade. It had been gnawing away at my consciousness, leading to an all-too-familiar sense of despair and hopeless, and trying to push itself forward from the deepest, oldest recesses of my mind.

The conversation explored the amazing adaptions of a woodpecker, my breathless admiration at the dazzling flash of a kingfisher, the secret life of the pine marten and anything else that took our fancy, the two gardaí as interested in the natural world as I was. Engrossed in past experiences, it was easy to forget I was travelling at speed, under arrest, to the capital city's criminal court for allegations that were, at best, untrue.

Thinking about the kingfishers brought another worry to mind: how was I to get home? I voice my concerns to my companions.

'Oh … we hadn't thought about that,' came the reply. 'Technically you can't travel back with us, because you'll no longer be under arrest and we're not allowed carry passengers,' the garda added.

The driver looked aghast. 'We can't just abandon him in the city – he's got a home to go to.'

'And don't forget my dog,' I added helpfully, trying not to sound overanxious.

'Don't worry,' he said, 'we'll sort something out – we'll get you home somehow. Let's get the other stuff out of the way first and we'll deal with that afterwards.'

I had started my day lit by a canvas of colour and filled with birdsong, fresh scents and air so crisp that you could taste it on your tongue. Ending the day in the criminal court was, by comparison, the polar opposite. Trying to find the door from the car park into the building itself was problematic, as it was a long time since either garda had been there. Exploring rows of doors, each of us tried one door after another, until finally one yielded. 'We're in,' came the relieved chorus.

Inside, the concrete-lined corridors, the convergence of echoing voices and the fluorescent lighting conspired to create a depressing and unwelcoming atmosphere that did nothing to lift the cloud that had resettled on me. More paperwork, transfer approval and processing ensued: another new, albeit friendly, face saying, 'Come on, let's get you sorted and out of here, this isn't a place for people like you.' Moments later, a judge listened attentively to the allegations that had been made against me, before saying, 'There's no case here; there's no evidence of any wrongdoing.'

In what felt like minutes, the rooms and corridors were emptied, and I was faced with the challenge of how to get back home. The gardaí who had accompanied me and sat opposite me in front of the judge were nowhere to be seen, nor did anyone else know of their whereabouts. The only suggestion was, 'Try the front door.' Since I had arrived using the 'tradesman's entrance' in the basement of a four-storey building, locating the 'front door' was not as easy as it sounded.

Finally, a helpful hand guided me into the lift with the instruction of taking it up to the second floor. As the lift doors opened for me to leave, I was greeted by the surprised faces of my two travelling companions. '*There* you are!' exclaimed one of them, 'We've been looking *everywhere* for you. Come on, let's get you out of here and home.'

It took not just their determination, but that of five more gardaí to figure out the logistics of that challenge.

Undoubtedly, many other people in such circumstances may have retreated to the nearest pub, or at the very least a coffee shop, to re-evaluate the day's injustice. However, I was in no mood for surrounding myself with yet more people. Navigating one of our country's highest courts had been both a pioneering and an exhausting process for me. If there was anywhere that I would have wanted to go afterwards, it would have been back to the river and surrounding oak woods. The sounds of dippers, kingfishers, great spotted woodpeckers – and even just the water chattering its rhythmical notes over the moss-covered stones – would have been the perfect antithesis to the day's stresses.

But it was now too late to consider returning to that particular oasis of calmness. However, the reassuring familiarity of my childhood home offered a secure sanctuary. There, many things, even persons, remained in my eyes unchanged. It was a place of safety and, perhaps more importantly, stability.

It was late evening, not long before sunset, when I reached my refuge. My mind had been on autopilot for most of the day, with my thoughts, actions and decisions guided and steered by those who had my best interests at heart. The intensity of the day had been overwhelming on so many levels. Despite this, I was still looking forward to my eventual return to the river the following day, and to discovering what the birds had been up to during my absence.

The following day, my stability restored, I returned to the beckoning river: however, it was late by the time I had organized myself enough to do so. I sat down on the track, a bit back from the river's edge. In front of me was a small weir, made from a line of stones, laid down by an unknown person at some point in the past. Dancing its way along this crazy pavement was a male grey wagtail, his plumage resplendent in the light of the setting sun. His sulphur-yellow underparts and ebony-black bib shimmered and flickered as he jived and pranced after the throngs of midges that swarmed low over the water. His long tail acted as a counterweight as he twisted, twirled and pirouetted his way towards me.

I envied his enthusiasm and his exuberance, both of which had now deserted me. The high spirits I had enjoyed on discovering the kingfishers' nest were now all but erased by the uncertainty I felt, that undefined and ambiguous fear of the unknown. The ability to look forward, and to reflect backward, is one of humankind's strengths – and weaknesses – an ability not shared by the bird I watched, which probably explained its joie de vivre.

Taking out my flask, I attempted to make a cup of tea using the last of the now-tepid water from this morning's knapsack. Although barely warm enough to infuse the tea leaves, it provided a welcome opportunity to sit, to watch and to listen. I loved this part of the river.

The noise of the water flowing over the weir provided a constant, welcome background noise: like an endless incantation, it helped quieten my mind. This noise made my world quieter.

However, the quietness of that world was shattered by the piercing whistle that announced the arrival of a kingfisher. Flying towards me from further downstream, its call heralded its approach long before I saw it. Seconds later, my eyes picked it up flying low over the water, tilting its body this way and that, before coming to land on one of the rocks that formed the weir in front of me. Hidden amongst the grass, unseen by its keen eyes, I was able to regard its plumage in intricate detail. Each of its blue feathers revealed itself to be composed of endless combinations of tints and shades within that one colour. But it was its bill that primarily drew my attention. Glistening in the sunlight, it was a uniform black – from the tiny hook on the end to where it met the dazzling iridescence of its plumage – clearly identifying this individual as a male.

He sat there in front of me, his small, squat shape; tiny, red feet; and black bill making him look not unlike a leprechaun. Bobbing his head up and down, at the same time he tilted it from side to side, looking first at the sky above him and then at the flowing river beneath him. He neither called nor searched for food; he simply sat there, alongside me, enjoying the last of the evening light.

Then, with no sound to herald his departure, he took off and flew back downstream, disappearing behind a bend in the river. I remained there as the darkness encroached. The first bats emerged from under the bridge, skimming low over the river ...

Silence, except for the occasional *plop* from a rising trout.

# THE SERPENT'S LAIR

THE PATTERN OF me sitting on the riverside and the kingfisher ensconced inside the riverbank – both of us hidden from view – was one that persisted for several weeks. Incubation is generally quite a predictable affair, unlike fledging, which varies considerably depending on food supply and can take up to three weeks. However, it is usually impossible to know when incubation has commenced, so I could never be certain when exactly the eggs might hatch.

Because both the male and female were so similar in appearance, it was often hard to know which of the pair was incubating at any given time. I knew both sexes shared the task, but it seemed that the female carried out the lion's share. Although the male certainly played a part, I felt that he did so only when the female needed to be relieved, which was not the case with the great spotted woodpeckers. In this species, the male willingly undertakes more than his fair share.

I found it fascinating that the evolution of birds has produced such fundamental differences in the behaviour of species. Evolution favours the development of an advantageous behaviour that makes the survival of a species more likely in a given environment. I would have thought that a single, most successful way to incubate eggs would have been settled long ago, yet the methods still vary considerably from species to species.

Birds such as robins and blackbirds employ a strategy where the female alone is responsible for incubation. Red-necked phalaropes – a small wading bird which is extremely rare in Ireland – have evolved to take the opposite approach, with only the male performing this duty. Others, such as the kingfishers and woodpeckers, share the workload, though not necessarily equally, and with the lion's share of the burden falling on different sexes. One task but many different solutions, all apparently equally successful.

While one of the parents was in the nest, the other ranged up and down along the river, sometimes feeding but more often just sitting doing nothing in particular. Unlike the dippers, where territories were often adjacent to one another, there were no other kingfishers nesting in the immediate vicinity. Because of this, there were no territorial disputes, and therefore little reason to endlessly patrol the river in search of intruders. It was a time of calmness and stillness, mirrored by both the watcher and the watched.

When I did see one of the pair, perched amongst the many overhanging branches along the river, it usually turned out to be the male, identified by his all-black bill. This is what led me to believe that the female undertook much of the incubation. Often the male was seen simply perched on a branch, close in against the riverbank, usually well hidden amongst the emergent leaves. The female, whenever she did put in an appearance, would often hunt actively and was usually much more alert and conspicuous. This suggested that the male had more time to spare and did not need to expend all of his energy outside of the nest hole on feeding.

At no time did I ever see the male carry a fish to the female while she was inside the burrow. Now that the courtship was finished, all the supplementary feeding and expressive presentation of fish that accompanied it had been abandoned also. Only on one occasion did I see the male arrive with a fish as a gift for his mate. I had been sitting there for almost half an hour with no sightings of either bird when the familiar whistle sounded upstream from where I sat.

The male arrived in a dazzling, rainbow-like flash of colour. As he landed on a rock in the middle of the river, I could clearly see the fish he held tightly in his bill. It was obviously very freshly caught, as it still wriggled and twitched in spite of his firm grip. Somehow, despite his large mouthful, he continued to call. The female landed alongside him, presumably having left the nest in response to his summons.

She began to adopt a submissive posture, holding out her wings in emulation of a begging youngster, gently calling as she solicited his affections. However, he failed to respond – at least straight away. She continued to crouch before him and plead, but he simply looked the other way and stood proudly to attention, his head and bill directed slightly skyward. Eventually he conceded and, turning around to face her, he repositioned the still-moving fish in his bill and presented it to her. She greedily grabbed it, and without a moment's hesitation the male flew back in the direction he had come from.

The female sat there for a short time, quietly bobbing her head and occasionally preening. The sunlight glinted off the pale rose tint of her bill before she took off and flew towards the hidden nest chamber. She hovered briefly in front of the brambles and ferns that shielded the burrow's entrance from my eyes, looking not unlike a giant hummingbird. Then she dipped down and disappeared under the vegetation. I caught a glimpse of blue behind the leaves as she entered the nest, and then she was gone.

The kingfishers were not the only birds along that stretch of river that were then sitting on eggs. Much of the river on which these kingfishers had chosen to nest was fast-flowing and strewn with rocks. The water surged and foamed through a series of mini-rapids, waterfalls and canyons. In some places the current slowed and became deeper, meandering through the extensively wooded valley like a large, fat snake. It was these deeper channels and sweeping, loop-shaped banks that were home to one of Wicklow's wariest birds – the goosander.

I was well hidden on the bank of the river, a line of gorse bushes shielding me from the water's edge. I love gorse. The yellow flowers are such a rich and vibrant colour, and from them emanates one of the most unusual and intoxicating scents of any Irish flower. It is the heady aroma of warm coconut – there is no other way to describe it – and on this calm, early summer morning it made the air smell like a tropical island. I watched the river in front of me, lying on my chest and peering through the dense, prickly vegetation, but there was no sign of my quarry. By now, I had been there for well over an hour and was starting to feel the effects of lying on the damp, uneven ground for so long – but patience is something every naturalist must learn if he or she wishes to experience the natural world and discover its secrets.

A movement on the water upstream caught my eye: a fleeting flash of grey and white on the surface, leaving nothing but a series of expanding ripples fading away to the opposite shore. I was scanning the river's surface when the sound of a splash made me turn my gaze – another series of expanding ripples. Had I been seen? Then a chestnut-coloured head, sporting a shaggy crest and a long, thin, red bill, popped up in the middle of the channel directly in front me: a female goosander.

The goosander is a species of duck, yet it is one that few people have even heard of, let alone seen. This is not surprising, considering that only about twenty-five or thirty pairs of this elusive species breed in Ireland. They were not recorded as a regularly breeding species in Ireland until the mid-1980s, but did occur as a vagrant from other countries, with the occasional pair remaining to breed. However, a small population, most likely originating from Wales, where the species is quite widespread, eventually established itself in the Wicklow Mountains.

Chiefly occurring on deep glaciated lakes and fast-flowing mountainous rivers, that small population has retained a tenuous hold there ever since. Despite numbers increasing slightly in the years immediately following those pioneers' arrival, thus far they have failed to expand much further. Their success, and their limitations, are due to them being highly specialized both when it comes to their feeding and their nesting requirements.

Goosanders belong to a group of ducks known as 'sawbills'. Their long, thin bills are edged with rows of sharp, backward-pointing ridges. These act somewhat like teeth, providing extra grip when catching the slippery fish which form the majority of their diet. They swim low to the water, their tapered bodies slicing through it like a submarine, negotiating rocks, rapids and weirs with ease.

The male is a most impressive-looking bird. His sharply defined, dark-coloured head, which looks almost black at a distance or in dull light, resolves to a deep bottle green when the light reflects off it. His steep forehead highlights his long and slender, blood-red bill, while the back of his head is frayed into a thick, shaggy, downward-pointing crest. His back is defined by a broad, black stripe extending from the neck to the wingtips. His flanks are a subtle shade of grey, like a wisp of smoke. Occasionally, for example when turning around in the water to preen, his vivid, orange legs add an unexpectedly vibrant flash of colour to what otherwise appears like a bird designed in the monochrome of a winter's day.

Like many other ducks, the female has no need for such ostentatious ornamentation. Caring for a nest full of eggs demands subdued patterning, not brashness. Her head is a rich chestnut and a grey wash defines her back, unlike the black sported by the male. The feathers on the back of her head form a short, shaggy crest, which the male lacks. She has evolved to blend in, whereas his striking plumage cries out to be noticed.

Goosanders are shy, secretive birds, spending most of their lives in pairs or in small groups of four or five birds. Their days are occupied by feeding on the quietest, most undisturbed and least accessible parts of the river. They usually feed close to the bank, swimming stealthily along with their heads underwater, looking for fish sheltering under the overhanging banks. This method of fishing is often referred to as 'snorkelling'. Goosanders seem mainly to dive once they have identified potential prey by snorkelling, rather than simply diving and then actively hunting, unlike so many other waterbird species, such as the cormorant.

Rarely do you see goosanders by design – chance encounters are the norm when it comes to this bird, usually while walking along a well-wooded stretch of river. During April and May, sightings are usually of single birds, often the male, guarding the territory as the female, hidden from view, incubates the eggs in the nest. Alternatively, it might be the female which is seen during one of her periodic, brief forays from the nest to feed. This solitary and secretive behaviour is something they share with the kingfishers, whose territory was also located on the same stretch of river.

However, there is one exception to the goosanders' normally solitary lifestyle and unpredictable nature, namely the dawn lek. A lek is a traditional location where male birds of a certain species gather, usually at first light, to perform courtship displays. Visiting females are enticed to choose a mate as the males vie for their attention by showing off their plumage and strength of character.

IT WAS FEBRUARY, an hour before sunrise, and it was bitterly cold. I was hidden on the shore of a lake in a spectacular glaciated valley. A mixture of oak, mountain ash and Scots pine covered the steeply sloping sides which rose out of the water. Higher up, far above me, the trees thinned out into scree-covered slopes, which then faded into a heather-carpeted skyline. This mosaic of habitats was reflected in the mirror-like surface of the deep water in front of me.

The sky was that distinguishing shade of blue that comes ahead of the sunrise, but it would be a while before the sun reached into this dark rift in the land. A mist hung low over the water, barely reaching more than a couple of metres skyward. It twisted and writhed like a living creature. Tortured, nebulous tendrils emerged from the pall above the water and dissipated into the expansiveness of the dawn sky. As the air temperature began to rise, the opacity of the veil shrouding the lake began to decrease and shapes started to emerge. Sleek and sinuous silhouettes moved in lines across the water, like a convoy of warships. More and more became visible as clarity and light filtered into the valley: goosanders.

For a few weeks in early spring, goosanders from surrounding river systems gather at dawn – not to feed, nor to roost, but rather to display and find a mate. Between twenty and thirty birds can be seen in a single morning, representing a large proportion of the Wicklow, and indeed Irish, breeding population. As is often the case with this species, the females outnumbered the males by a considerable margin. In a group of twenty birds it would not be unusual to see no more than six or seven adult males. On this particular morning, there were only five.

Line upon line of female goosanders swam ever closer, each flotilla accompanied by one or two males intent on securing a mate. Clearly it was a case of 'ladies' choice' in this dance. The males vied for attention, throwing their bottle-green heads backwards with an upward flick of their crimson bills. Strange, guttural moans emanated from these ghostly shapes and carried across the still waters. The females were oblivious to these performances by the males and, paying little courtesy, merely swam around preening.

Occasionally a male would try his luck with one of the other groups and approach the attendant male with his head and neck stretched out low along the water. His torpedo-shaped profile sped across the water – orange paddles thrashing the water behind – as he powered himself towards his opponent. The moans were now replaced with more aggressive-sounding growls and grunts. As the glass-like water surface was churned up by the pursuing males, the females ceased their preening and started flapping their way across the water towards a quieter part of the lake.

This hectic game of chasing and courting takes place each morning for several weeks during spring and is the sole reason the birds gather here in a large group, the only time of year they do so in such numbers. As the sun began its rise on this particular morning, still hidden by the high valley walls, the brightening sky signalled a change in their behaviour. They swam closer and closer towards my hiding place behind the bank of gorse bushes. Soon they were mere metres in front of me, every feather, every subtle marking clearly visible. The males, seen up close, have a pink blush across their white breasts, a feature only seen during this short period of courtship. The females' grey flanks are transformed into a delicate pattern of crescents, chevrons and vermiculations set against a cream background – an artist's dream.

Having reached the shore in front of me, they all turned around as one and took off, flying towards the far end of the valley. Steadily climbing upwards, they gained height, and by the time they reached the far end they were half the height of the U-shaped valley walls. Turning around again, still gaining altitude, they flew towards where I was sitting. By the time they had flown over me, they had reached a sufficient height that they could escape the valley and disperse into the numerous river systems which cut through the area.

As they flew overhead, mere specks against the blue firmament, they resembled a formation of fighter planes – twenty-five sleek arrow silhouettes in a diamond-shaped formation disappeared in seconds. The group would now split up into smaller parties and secret themselves away on undisturbed waterways until the following morning's gathering. Today's show was over.

The female goosander now swimming in front of me had probably not frequented that mountain lake in several months. Having chosen her mate, the pair had ceased visiting the lek many weeks prior, as undoubtedly had all the other goosanders, to seek out a territory in which to nest. In common with the neighbouring kingfishers, which were nesting in the bank not too far upstream, they also had an unusual choice of nest site – so unusual, in fact, that it was unique amongst Irish ducks: high up in a tree.

Warily, she swam past me, her body so low in the river that the water washed over her back. Rivulets and droplets glistened like beads of molten silver as they slid effortlessly off her waterproof feathers. Her head and neck emerged from the surface like a periscope. Time and time again she dived, to resurface, half-submerged, further down the river. She was not feeding, but rather surveying the area for predators before revealing the location of her nest. Goosanders, like kingfishers, are hole-nesters, but they use natural holes rather than excavating their own.

Unlike other Irish ducks, which favour nesting on the ground, goosanders favour large holes in trees. These usually occur where a bough has been torn from the trunk, allowing a cavity to form through decay. Because the goosander is quite a large duck, this cavity must be quite substantial if it is to hold both the female and her nest. And therein lies one of the limiting factors for the increase of this species: suitable nest sites. Tall trees by the river's edge containing natural cavities are not a common occurrence – but this bird was fortunate.

On the bank opposite me was a majestic and towering Douglas fir: a magnificent specimen, it stood proudly in its isolation. Symmetrically balanced and geometrically perfect, its conical form towered above the single trunk that anchored its massive body to the earth. As the goosander swam closer towards it, she cocked her head to one side so that she could focus an eye clearly on its crown. Satisfied there was no sign of predators, either in the fir or the surrounding water, she took off and flew up to the top of the tree.

Landing on a branch some twenty metres above the ground, she presented an unusual sight, and one not normally associated with ducks. She sat there, preening momentarily, while a blue tit scolded her angrily. Small woodland birds such as this would not be accustomed to a large duck unexpectedly landing alongside them. Her toilette finished, she waddled along the branch, one orange foot either side of the limb, until she disappeared amongst the foliage. Due to the tree's height and the density of the needles, I was unable to see either the nest cavity or even its location. However, I did know from many days' observations that it would be several hours before she reappeared. I wondered what her nest was like …

SEVERAL DAYS LATER, I was standing below the Douglas fir with a local wildlife ranger. I gazed upwards at the towering pinnacle above my head.

'Are you really going to climb this?' I asked my companion.

'Of course,' she replied, 'it's a straightforward climb.'

Because of their scarcity and small breeding population, nesting goosanders in Wicklow are closely monitored by the National Parks and Wildlife Service (NPWS). Accessing the nest is carried out under licence by trained professionals with specialist skills, chiefly mountain climbing with ropes.

Using a catapult, a weight with a line attached was shot over the topmost boughs of the tree, above the nest site. This line was then used to feed a stronger climbing rope over the bough and back down to the ground. Clipping the rope safely to her harness, my companion began her ascent and scaled the tree with ease. After negotiating a course around a few challenging branches and broken spurs, it was not long before she reached the crown and the densest part of the foliage.

Being terrified of heights, I knew I would never get to see into a goosander's nest. Even looking over a vertical drop of two or three metres will cause knots in my stomach and trigger that anxious, sinking feeling deep in my bowels. In situations like this, I was happy merely to be the observer. Having reached the top, the climber gently parted the foliage and shouted down, 'She's away from the nest, probably feeding, and she's covered the eggs.'

The nest was in a cleft in the trunk and was thickly lined with copious quantities of soft down, plucked by the female from her own breast. When leaving the nest to feed, which she does several times a day, she covers the eggs with a layer of down to keep them warm until her return. Only the female carries out the three-week long incubation, unlike the situation with kingfishers, where both sexes share the workload.

There were twelve eggs in this clutch, but it is not unusual to have up to fourteen. The eggs were the same size as a hen's egg and a light buff olive in colour. Everything checked and noted, the climber abseiled back down the tree in a fraction of the time it had taken to ascend. Quickly, ropes and other equipment were removed from the site, and we melted into the woodland before the female returned to the tree.

LATER THAT EVENING, I returned to make sure all was well. As I watched from behind the row of gorse bushes, I saw the male drifting down the river like a brightly coloured model boat. The evening sunlight illuminated the iridescence of his head, which exploded across the river in dazzling shards and points of light and colour. A beadlet of water hung from the sharp, hooked tip of his bill, tentatively balancing and challenging gravity, before breaking free and dropping onto the river's surface with the tiniest of splashes.

As he drew level with me, he turned his head and started preening the black feathers on his back. Pulling each one in turn through his serrated bill, he smoothed them out and ensured they were in perfect condition. While doing so, the female flew unannounced from the nest and landed nearby on the river, her feet shattering the perfect mirrored reflection of the surrounding woodland into shards of chaotic turbulence. She swam over to her mate, who greeted her arrival with a throaty chuckle. The two birds continued to preen as they slowly began to drift downstream. All was well in their world.

Unlike with many of the other birds I had studied on this river, much of the goosanders' breeding behaviour is hard to observe. There is often little to be seen, save for the female's arrival and departure. The male rarely puts in an appearance, and when the female emerges, she often flies several hundred metres from the tree in order to feed. Often all that is gained over the course of a day are a few brief flight views and perhaps the occasional sighting of a bird on the river.

Once the ducklings hatch, they leave the nest within twenty-four hours and travel on the river with their mother. Within a day they might relocate hundreds of metres from their nest, making it almost impossible to follow them and watch their development over the subsequent weeks. Compared to birds such as great spotted woodpeckers, which provide ample opportunities for study at the nest, much of the goosanders' lifestyle in Ireland is shrouded in mystery.

The occasional encounters I have had with goosander families, after they have embarked on their journey from the nest, have never included the father. The males seem to head off on a solitary quest of their own, abandoning their ducklings' natal territory and spending their days cruising alongside the riverbanks alone. Often, during high summer, I have unexpectedly come across solitary males along stretches of the river on which I would previously have sighted goosanders.

These lone males are often far more approachable at this time of year. Sometimes, when sitting on the bank, one might float past me, completely unbothered by my presence. Steaming along like a cruise liner, his brightly coloured and contrastingly marked plumage gleams in the strong, midsummer sunshine like the hull of a freshly painted boat. The riverbank's rich and vibrant greenery, bedecked with an array of multicoloured summer flowers, forms an astoundingly beautiful backdrop to this unique and delightful duck.

By comparison, the females and their young become very secretive. They seek out those stretches of riverbank shaded by overhanging and invasive laurels and rhododendrons. The glossy leaves often trail in the water, like a hand reaching over the side of a rowing boat. Dark and shady fissures and cavities form in the dense foliage, and it is there where the female hides her youngsters.

Protectively positioned just on the edge of the overgrowth, the female fights against the current to keep alongside the ducklings, sheltering out of view under the branches. To the uninitiated eye, she is simply a grey-bodied duck with a chestnut head, just sitting there. But every few minutes, small, yellow-and-brown-striped fluffballs scoot out and swim around, like a cohort of wind-up clockwork toys, before she chases them safely back under the leaves and out of sight. She doesn't need to teach them how to feed or swim, she only needs to protect them against predators such as American minks, otters and grey herons.

Such a secretive lifestyle, played out along many kilometres of variably accessible rivers, means that it is hard to know how many pairs breed, where their nests are and how many chicks from the average-sized brood of twelve survive into adulthood. The springtime gathering on the glaciated valley lakes is often the only opportunity to see the birds in any sort of number, but this only provides a population estimate that is, at best, tenuous. However, although spring is the best time to see them displaying, it is not the only time they gather there.

LATE OCTOBER AND the wind was cutting through the valley with a bite like an enraged animal. The water was being whipped into wavelets, which were then driven the length of the valley before crashing onto the sandy shore in front of me. The spindrift spewed into foamy, frothy bubbles that blew past me, landing and exploding like balloons on the spines of the gorse bushes.

The surface of the lake was a maelstrom of broken, dark reflections and white-topped waves, a pattern of light and dark, constantly changing – sometimes pleasing, sometimes not, but always distracting. Above, the high ridges of the valley sides shone as they caught the first reachings of the sun. At the far end of the lake lay a distant sand bar, formed by the deposition of countless years' erosion of the surrounding granite by a river that coursed down the slopes at the head of this valley. Sitting on the sandbar was a large group of goosanders.

Half-hidden by the lake's whitecaps, which ruffled the surface into an endless range of miniature mountain peaks, I counted one bird after another, some preening, some sleeping, some simply sitting in the dull light: one, two, ten, fourteen … There were at least twenty-one birds, maybe more, since many were only barely visible. Through my telescope I saw only two males, but several birds, which otherwise resembled females, had more white on them than expected. Others had less-clear demarcations in their female-like plumage.

I realized that, unlike the spring gathering of adult birds, this autumn gathering was a family affair. The parents and their youngsters, now fully grown but still moulting into adult plumage, were gathering as a social group. This was the first time I had seen this behaviour amongst goosanders, and it proved that – for the time being, at least – many of the youngsters had survived those difficult first months of life and were now approaching independence. Whether there was one family there on that beach or the offspring from several families, I would never know. And, although the population of this fascinating species was small, it was safe to assume that many chicks from the mere handful of Wicklow's nesting pairs did in fact survive.

Throughout my exploration of the river systems in search of kingfishers, I encountered goosanders in many different locations and at different times of year. All were memorable, but one sighting stands out above them all. Every encounter is unique: sometimes new behaviour is noted, other times a plumage detail is spotted for the first time. These are reminiscent of the close-up examinations of a painting, rather than standing back and looking at the overall canvas ...

IT WAS MIDWINTER, and I was returning along the edge of the same lake where I had fruitlessly been searching for kingfishers. The winter sun, lacking in warmth, had already set and left a cold, powder-blue sky, rapidly darkening towards indigo and foretelling sub-zero temperatures. We were cold, myself and my dog, but the experience of evenfall beckoned us, promising serenity and countering the anxiety of the coming days. Leaving the wooded track, we wound our way to the lakeside and sat at the water's edge. The silence was almost complete, as was the stillness, both of the world and of my mind.

The valley wall opposite rose darkly from the shadowy waters. No colour was discernible, merely monochrome. The ridgetop was clearly defined against the pale sky, as though an artist had painted it with India ink. The water, a perfect looking glass, did not just reflect the scene – it rivalled it. So perfect was this inverse world that it was almost impossible to tell where reality ended and contemplation began; it was possible to lose yourself in a world of your own making.

Over the ridge, the cold moon hung trembling in the still, cooling air. Its counterpart looked up from the opaque water surface. A single sound pierced the silence that partly defined this gloaming: a guttural quacking. Looking to my left, two shapes emerged from the almost-complete darkness, their silhouettes crisply etched into the sky. Like an image of a pair of Chinese dragons, with their long, thin necks and rakish bills, the two goosanders began to lose altitude as they approached.

Still calling, they held their wings up and stretched out their webbed feet as they prepared to land. These paddles smashed the perfection into millions of rippling shards and slivers, shattering the moon, destroying the landscape and creating noise from silence.

Completely unaware of our presence – myself and my dog had simply become part of the landscape – they slowly swam in front of us. The disturbed waters calmed ... waves slowing to ripples ... before finally fading into flatness. The two birds gently swam into a silvery, rippling pool of moonlight before cutting a line across the moon's reflected face. As they left the cold beam of light and entered the deepening darkness along the cliffs, disappearing into obscurity, I realized that nightfall was now almost complete.

With the arrival of night, the silence was broken. Not with birdsong – for it would be many hours before any songbirds awoke – but with an eerie, long-drawn-out wail. It was similar to the sound made by blowing up a balloon and then slowly letting the air out. It went from being a high-pitched whistle to a low, bass-heavy moan, as though the air had run out. If heard from closer by, it would have raised the hairs along both our necks, yet it was nothing to be scared of. It was the sound of a sika deer stag proclaiming his domain. Rutting season. Marking the start of a busy night's work for him, it signalled the fireside for us.

The pattern of the kingfishers' incubation continued much the same each day. Regardless of the time of day, weather conditions or duration of my stay, their behaviour was similar and, to a degree, predictable. Sometimes I would encounter the non-incubating bird as I made my way along the bank towards the nest site – a blaze of blue suddenly exploding from a riverside tree and speeding away, before being lost to view around a bend in the river.

Other times I would arrive unnoticed, and quite some time would pass before either bird appeared. Rarely, however, would I see a changeover: that moment when a bird arrived to relieve its mate from its cramped, dark entombment. With woodpeckers it was a predictable affair, which took place about every half-hour. One bird would suddenly land unannounced on the tree alongside the entrance hole.

This immediately prompted the incubating bird to leave, allowing the other to quickly enter. So fast was the changeover that it only took seconds to complete.

The kingfishers employed a more leisurely approach. Sometimes a bird exited with no sign of its mate and disappeared along the river. In these cases, it was hard to know whether the bird that returned to the nest soon thereafter was the same individual that had just left or not. Other times it would only emerge in response to a summoning whistle, usually from the male. Only on one occasion did they behave in a manner similar to that of the woodpeckers.

I had arrived that morning and watched the nest for an hour, but there was no sign of either bird. Then one appeared, as though out of nowhere, hovering in front of the brambles that screened the nest. I was unable to see which of the pair it was, since the bird's head was turned away from me. As it continued to hover there, gently moving from side to side like a softly swaying leaf, its mate inside the burrow slipped quietly out from under the brambles and flew down the river.

The first bird continued to hover, its whirring wings a blur of blue, before it dipped down and up into the nest, disappearing from view. Neither bird had called, nor had they acknowledged each other in any way that I had perceived. This changing of the guard was as discreet and perfectly timed as could be executed. Yet, for all my watching, it felt like the exception rather than norm – for this nest, at any rate.

With each passing week of observation, I knew I was closer to the young chicks hatching. I may not have known what date they started to incubate, but it had to be less than three weeks from when I first realized that they were sitting on the eggs. By the time two weeks had passed, I knew that the chicks could quite literally hatch any day now, and I always arrived full of expectation – and left filled with the same. Although I was unable to commit hours upon hours to my pursuit, I usually managed to observe the nest at least once each day, and more often two or three times daily.

IT WAS LATE one evening during the third week of May when I arrived to find that things had changed. I had made my way along the river, pausing only to watch the grey wagtail and dipper families, when a kingfisher sped past me. Surprisingly, it was flying in the same direction as I was headed – towards the nest. The evening sunlight revealed a paleness to the bird's bill. As a consequence, I assumed this had to be the female. When I arrived at the nest, there was no sign of either bird, so I quickly set up my makeshift hide and settled in under my sheet.

Only a few minutes later a kingfisher came around the bend in the river upstream, alighting on a broken branch close to the nest. I could clearly see that this was the male and that he had a fish clasped firmly in his beak. I waited for the female to emerge and receive his offering, but she failed to appear. Taking off, he flew up towards the nest and disappeared under the brambles and into the burrow. Moments later he re-emerged, minus the fish, and returned to the branch. After a quick preen he flew back up the river, calling as he went. No sooner was he gone than the female alighted on that same branch, also carrying a fish. Mirroring the male's behaviour, she flew into the nest and then back out onto the branch, before flying up the river after her mate ...

The chicks had hatched.

# DESCENT INTO DARKNESS

WE ALL HAVE 'bad' days. Days when nothing goes according to plan, when small things appear ridiculously dramatic or result in what is, to others, a completely inappropriate response. But today was different. Often, while setting out to search for my kingfishers, I had great expectations. Perhaps I would see them mating? Or maybe an intruding male would initiate a squabble that would dramatically escalate into a fight to the death? And then, disappointingly, I would reach the day's end and have failed to see a kingfisher at all. In other words, if my day had not gone according to plan, it was a 'bad' day. But this was different. This was worse.

Now that the kingfishers' eggs had hatched, I was preparing myself for some serious observations. If this was to be anything like the woodpeckers or dippers, I could expect to see the adult birds returning every ten or fifteen minutes, offering continuous and hopefully prolonged views.

With the weather becoming more favourable at the onset of June and its associated long hours of daylight, things had finally fallen into place. The prospect of spending a considerable amount of time surrounded by nature and indulging myself with the kingfishers' private life was delightful. It was the perfect antithesis to the dark clouds and despondency that had threatened me weeks beforehand. A marked downturn, which had followed me ever since.

The next day I realized it was going to be far warmer than expected. I was travelling with my dog, who often slept in the car while I was away. I did not want to leave her too long, even in the shade, so decided on a short visit. Having arrived at the nest, I quickly disappeared under the safety of my makeshift hide. The lilting whispers of the river and the gentle movement of air through the leaves above me were the only sounds. However, the stillness did not last long.

As I sat under my bedsheet on the bank of the river, I stared at the vibrating screen of the phone for what felt like an eternity, but in reality was only seconds. 'Gardaí' flashed across the screen in vibrant, neon red, set against an onyx-black background. But to my overactive mind, racing like a McLaren out of control on a racetrack, it read, 'Your life is changing.' So I answered it.

'Good morning,' I began, 'how can I help you this time?'

It wasn't the same garda as last time, but this one was just as helpful. 'I was wondering if you could call down to us?' she said. 'We've a few questions we need to ask you.'

Not again, I thought to myself. I really could have done without this intrusion. I had arranged my whole day to enable me to spend a small amount of time with the kingfishers. I did not want my schedule being unnecessarily reorganized. I had everything planned for a day's study. Time was of the essence. The birds' behaviour changed and developed all the time, and I couldn't afford to waste it sleeping or eating, and certainly not entertaining other people's problems. For the thousandth time, I wondered why I couldn't just be left alone. All I wanted – in fact, all I asked for – was to embrace the world around me while sharing it with my dog. Why was that so hard?

'What is it *this* time?' I asked the garda.

'There's been an allegation made against you,' she said. 'However,' she added, 'as far as I can tell, it seems to be just another misunderstanding, the same as last time.' Perhaps she had not been updated, I thought, or perhaps she was looking at the dates incorrectly? Either way, I felt that the least I could do was to enlighten her. I told her that we had already dealt with that in court and that the judge had simply dismissed the charge with a wave of his hand.

'No,' she said, 'even if it is a misunderstanding, it is still a fresh allegation, and a more complicated one.'

I listened in disbelief to the details of the complaint. As she recounted them, I was distracted by the chinking call of a dipper nearby and turned to look.

There was one of the youngsters sitting on a rock in front of me at the water's edge. It was frantically flapping its wings and stretching its neck forward as it called incessantly. Its high-pitched cries were directed at one of its parents, which was foraging several metres away. It always fascinated me how the over-the-top, excited behaviour of these fledglings failed to elicit any urgency from the adult birds.

I was fairly sure it was the male bird in front of me, judging by its size, and he carried on searching under the stones for the larvae his offspring was desperately demanding. I could see no sign of the other sibling that usually accompanied the adult; perhaps its appetite had been satisfied.

I was wondering how much longer it would be before the young birds became independent, when a voice asked, 'So, where exactly are you now?'

'What?' I replied. 'Oh, right … hmm, well, to be honest, I'm kind of in the middle of something. Can't this wait?'

'No,' she said, 'we need you to come in here. I'm sorry to say this, but we need to arrest you again.'

I was confused. Obviously, I had become completely distracted by the dippers while the garda had been talking and had zoned out.

'But why?' I asked. My logical and factually thinking mind kicked into overdrive. I had done nothing wrong. I had abided by the law, to the letter. I was in the right, and therefore everybody else was in the wrong.

'Look,' I calmly continued, 'whatever has been said is basically lies, fabrication and harassment. You know that, I know that and the judge has already said something similar in relation to the previous false allegations. Can you not just sort it out yourselves and leave me out of this? I really *am* quite busy today.'

'I'm sorry,' she replied. 'Like we said before, we have no discretion when it comes to allegations of this sort. Only the judge can sort this out. Our hands are actually tied in matters such as these.' I sat and thought for a moment. Surely we wouldn't have to go back to the Central Criminal Court in Dublin again? And I had my dog in the car this time as well. How was that going to work?

I discussed the logistics of the arrest procedure with the garda. She was confident that if I presented myself straight away that morning then they could manage to arrange a special sitting of the local district court that afternoon and avoid having to make the trip to the Dublin courthouse. I really had no desire to return to that dismal environment and told her so.

'So, will you come into us straight away then?' she asked.

I decided not to try to explain why I was sitting under a bedsheet on a riverbank, nor that I really felt that the behaviour of these kingfishers was of more importance than these allegations – after all, the allegations could be dealt with at any stage, whereas the birds had a timetable. Most important was the fact that I was over a kilometre away from my car, in which sat a dog who had not yet had her morning walk.

Instead, I explained that as I hadn't planned on being arrested that day, it would take a while to get a few things organized, but that I would be there in about an hour or so. Then I remembered I hadn't had much breakfast and that garda stations weren't cafés. 'I also need to grab a Danish and a cappuccino,' I said, 'but that won't take long.'

Neither of the kingfishers had put in an appearance during our conversation, and both the adult dipper and its offspring flew off downstream as I threw off my makeshift hide. In the same way that a butterfly chrysalis splits open and the transformed caterpillar emerges into a new world, so I stepped out from under my bedsheet ...

But the 'new' world I stepped into was darker, the colours had lost their vibrancy and the surrounding orchestra of birdsong sounded harsh and unpleasant. I could no longer find anything of interest in the two birds flying away from me. And, as I looked at the natural world around me, it failed to arouse anything at all in me. Yes, we can all have 'bad' days. But this was different.

I like a predictable, well-ordered world. I don't embrace change well and am more at ease with routine and structure. Despite being quite sociable, I often find interacting with people challenging, which is why I retreat into nature, preferring the company of animals to people. Because I find comfort in things being just how I wish them to be, I organize the environment around me in the same manner, putting coping mechanisms in place and existing in my own world.

But now that world was changing, and I was being driven out of my comfort zone into a surreal existence: a world where all my carefully laid life plans began to crumble and collapse around me. And not just my plans, but the whole way in which I had arranged and organized my behaviour was now beginning to fall to pieces. I perceived the world in a way that didn't seem to match others' expectations, and the result of that was a force that rose against me and challenged me for doing nothing – nothing apart from spending time with my dog and exploring *my* world around me.

I struggled against this force, in the same manner as a small fish struggles when held fast in a kingfisher's bill, or a salmon fights against the current as it strives to return to its birthplace. They never give up, not if they wish to survive. The salmon doesn't stop swimming just because the rapids that lie ahead are too formidable – to do so is to accept defeat, to lie down and die. But to struggle against a force that endlessly parries, thrusts and thwarts is a battle with the odds stacked against you. And in this surreal world, a world not of my making and as alien to me as a dry riverbed is to a fish ... I never stood a chance.

This was not just a 'bad' day. This was different.

This was Kafkaesque.

There was no sound to be heard other than that of the flowing water. I remained on the riverbank for some time after I had finished the call with the garda. Part of me still wanted to push on in the quest for the river's soul, if only for the hope that it might lead away from this world – from this uncertainty, this unpredictability, this chaos and, possibly most of all, this noise.

I slowly gathered my equipment and began to pack up my bag. A familiar whistle caught my ear and, turning around, I watched a bolt of blue zipping downstream. I watched without interest, not even raising my binoculars to identify which of the pair it was or whether it was carrying food. I watched with no thought in my head, past, present or future. I felt removed from the world, a world that for the first time in my life appeared grey and uninteresting.

I was not without feeling or emotion on account of what had just transpired during my conversation with the garda, but the emotions that had been kindled, if that was what they were, were new ones. I was unfamiliar with the feelings that were spreading within me, and indeed had been for some time. As yet, I had no name with which to identify them. Unlike anger or joy, which regularly visited my mind by jumping in and out and all about, these gave the impression of an unwelcome visitor coming to stay.

I made my way back through the bankside vegetation, pushing through ranks of musky meadowsweet and rapidly unfurling bracken fronds. Eventually I reached my car and decided the first and most important task was to take my dog for a walk. Everything else could wait. Everything. The world was not going to end just yet.

AN HOUR AND three-quarters later I was parked outside the garda station. It was a paid parking area and I couldn't decide if I needed to pay – surely if you were under arrest you couldn't get a parking fine? I eventually decided that since I had been ordered to come here, I should not have to pay for the privilege and, leaving my dog in the car, went into the station.

The garda who greeted me was obviously unaware of the situation, and the conversation went much the same as it had the last time.

'Good morning, can I help you?' she enquired.

'Well,' I replied, 'I think you're looking to arrest me again.'

She stared and me with a puzzled expression and asked, 'For any particular reason?'

'Oh, I'm sure there's a reason,' I replied, 'but I haven't been told what it is yet. Why don't you ask the other gardaí if anyone is waiting for my arrival?' I suggested.

She stared at me for a moment in what appeared to be disbelief. Then, after taking my name and details, she closed the hatch, leaving me once more standing alone in the foyer.

I waited, but nothing happened for some time. Obviously, despite having previously been rushed to the Central Criminal Court, I was still not considered a major threat to society or a wanted criminal. Perhaps I should just return to the river, I thought.

It was a while before the door into the office finally opened and two pleasant-looking gardaí waved me inside. We went into the interview room and began getting stuck into the paperwork detailing the allegations, the charges and what we were going to do to resolve the issue.

'What took you so long to get here anyway?' one asked. 'We called you nearly two hours ago.'

My mind started processing at a ridiculously fast rate, switching off in the process. They hardly wanted to hear about the kingfisher nest and the fact I had to hike along the river to get there. I was also fairly sure that telling them I had taken my dog for a walk was not what they wanted to know either, nor the fact that she was outside in the car …

'The car,' I suddenly blurted out. 'Do I need to get a ticket for the car if you're arresting me?'

I was met with a double-blank stare. I quickly explained, to their astonishment, that I had parked outside with no ticket and had left the dog there.

'Well, you'll have to get someone to collect her,' came the response. I explained to them that since it was a working day, everyone who knew her was either working, not answering my calls or making allegations against me.

'We'll come back to her,' the older garda kindly said. His younger colleague smiled as she went through the issues facing us.

'Look, I know we've been through this before and you're probably frustrated. And no doubt it's distressing, but we come across these events all the time. Like all legal issues, it is just a matter of going through the rigmarole of processing and procedure. The quicker we do this,' she said, 'the quicker we all get back to where we were.'

Both gardaí were still hopeful I would be able to appear before a special sitting in the local district court, so things wouldn't take too long once we were given the go-ahead. They decided that once I was formally charged and arrested, I could move my car from the public car-parking spaces into a garda-designated parking area. It seemed ironic that I was going to be arrested and then sent outside to move my car, but the system is there for a reason, apparently.

As soon as I moved my car, I was left with the dilemma of my canine friend. I went back into the station and told the gardaí that, under arrest or not, I really needed to let her out for a bathroom break. There was a silence in the station as the two colleagues looked around at each other.

'It probably wasn't the best idea to bring her,' came a tentative voice.

'Well, we're not going anywhere until she's sorted,' I shot back.

A discussion followed, and a garda accompanied me around to the back of the station where a small, grassy area provided an opportunity of relief for my dog.

Feeling somewhat more relaxed thanks to this slight return to normality, I chatted to the garda as I played with my dog's ears. We discussed birds: woodpeckers, red kites and, inevitably, my quest for the kingfisher. Like most people, deep down he had an appreciation for nature, but life and work prevented him from being anything other than a passenger. Even in the midst of this surreal situation that he was trying to figure out, he was just doing his job, and for that I felt no frustration towards him.

I put my dog back on her lead and turned to go back to the car. Whether he saw how relaxed my dog was making me, or simply knew how best to manage a person like myself in stressful situations such as this, I don't know. But as we began to walk, he turned to me and said, 'Bring her inside if you like.'

'Really?' I said, staring at him in surprise.

We went back into the station and, much to my joy, the other gardaí were delighted to see her and made a fuss over her, before saying that both of us should wait in the interview room while they tried to arrange my court appearance.

There cannot be too many dogs that have spent an afternoon in custody, sitting alongside their friend while under arrest, but that is what she did, and I was just glad to have her there. More paperwork was processed, involving questions about medical history, medications and dietary requirements and whether I was taking Class A drugs ...

I continued to stroke my Dalmatian's ears and her muzzle, wondering if this would ever reach a conclusion. The more questions that were asked, the more surreal a world I felt I was in, and thoughts of losing emotional control loomed closer and closer. But, just as Peter was the rock on which Jesus built his church, so my dog was the rock that I clung to while the storm-driven waves of this bizarre situation crashed around me, threatening to destroy and drown me.

Eventually everything appeared to be in order, and we just needed to wait for confirmation of a court sitting. Whether because of my dog or not, or perhaps some other reason, they decided not to put me into a cell while under arrest this time and, after ensuring that I had everything I needed, they left us alone in the interview room.

During my previous visit to this station I had briefly visited the cells while awaiting preparations for travelling to Dublin. It was not the most pleasant of environs, and I was relieved that this time I was allowed to wait with my dog in a more normal setting. With fewer distractions, my mind roamed free and my thoughts returned to the flowing river – rippling, dancing and laughing over the sun-sparkled stones.

Many kingfishers reportedly raise two, sometimes even three, broods in a year. This is a strategy that has apparently evolved to combat the relatively high mortality rate of the chicks in the first few weeks of leaving the nest. In parts of Great Britain, kingfishers often breed from early March onwards and into August. This does not seem to be the case in Ireland, but definitive breeding data on this species was hard to come by. I was quite satisfied that my kingfishers were only on their first brood and in theory could easily have a second brood, but that would take them well into August, possibly September. This pair had certainly started to breed in March which, as the literature suggested, was most typical. Clearly, the breeding behaviour of birds in Ireland differed from those on the other side of the Irish Sea.

Even though I had a nest under observation, I really longed to find one that was not obscured by dense vegetation, one that would allow me a more detailed insight into the kingfishers' lives. Should I widen the net, so to speak? There was still plenty of time remaining during this breeding season to search for another, possibly more easily observed, nest. However, doing so would mean spending less time on the riverbank watching this pair. I was torn between decisions when my reverie was unexpectedly broken.

'OK, let's go, we've got a court hearing organized,' called out one of the gardaí. 'Oh – your dog!' was his next utterance.

They assured me this would not take long and that I would be free as soon as bail had been set, but then I thought back to the recent episode involving the Central Criminal Court.

'If I leave her in the car,' I said, 'how will I get back?'

'Don't worry,' they replied, 'we'll bring you back afterwards ourselves this time.' With my priorities sorted, we headed off for the district court in the garda car, easily negotiating the building Friday traffic by using lights and siren.

Once there, it didn't take long to read out the charges, assign a hearing date and set bail. In no time at all we were on our way back, having picked up an additional garda, who needed a lift on the way. Inevitably, with a new participant, the conversation in the car found its way around to woodpeckers and kingfishers once again. It was not long before we arrived back at the station, where a friendly spotted face was anxiously looking out of my car window.

Thankfully, we had not travelled into the city centre like last time, so a lot less of my day had been wasted. I had spent too much time listening to too many people and could barely remember half of what had been said. I needed space. The garda in the station made a few phone calls. Despite my wanting to return to the riverside straight away, my brother Gerry decided that returning to my home in Blackrock was a far safer option for both myself and my dog. After a period of downtime and assuring both him and the rest of my family of my well-being, we returned to the realm of the kingfisher.

I WAS GLAD finally to be back where I had planned to spend the day, but so much had changed, and in such a short space of time. I stared at the river meandering through the oakwood. The shadows of the trees had now lengthened in the evening sun, stretching their elongated and twisted shapes across the water like the tentacles of some monstrous creature lurking in the woods behind me.

I found it hard to concentrate and to remain enthusiastic and excited about my quest. The events of the day had left me drained, and despite them now being behind me, I could not seem to move forward. The years I had spent watching the woodpeckers had passed without incident and with anonymity – I had assumed this year would be no different. How I had ended up in a chain of events that were reshaping how I lived was a mystery to me.

The kingfisher may have had nothing to do with it, but in my mind it had become hopelessly involved, and would forever act as a marker to those events. Our minds are a great evolutionary achievement. Millions upon millions of neurons conveying thoughts, ideas and feelings at lightning-fast speeds. Neurons branching out like a fluvial fan, forming an intertwining net that covered an area larger than a football pitch.

But the mind could also be a trap, and it was possible to become lost in it. Sometimes, for reasons beyond our control, it loses the ability to balance the thoughts and emotions it experiences each day.

It 'forgets' that the sun rises each morning and only remembers this disc of hope gradually slipping below the horizon. I knew that to move forward I needed to see the sun rise and illuminate the world around me. That would take time, so I was told.

ONE AFTERNOON I was returning along the river, having spent the morning watching the woodpecker family, when I surprised a female sika deer near the river's edge. She bounded across the river, which was easily fordable at that point, and stood looking at me from the opposite bank. She had lost her dull, dark winter coat and now sported a beautiful, spotted pelt that glowed a mixture of chestnut, walnut and hazelnut tones. Her black-and-white tail flicked sideways in agitation as her liquid amber eyes watched me nervously.

I waited for her to bolt into the woods on the other side of the river, but strangely she stood her ground and continued watching me. Then she started bleating anxiously, and I noticed a small calf at the water's edge on my side of the river. It was no more than a day old, and I smiled to myself as it staggered along the grassy riverbank. Images of *Bambi* came to mind, and I had to agree with Thumper's famous observation: 'He's kinda wobbly, isn't he?'

The calf quivered his away along the riverbank, crying out to his mother, who watched apprehensively. As he tested the water with his tiny cloven hooves, she jumped back into the current and crossed to give aid. Nudging him with her nose and reassuring him, she encouraged him into the water and across the river onto the bank on the other side. I watched them through my binoculars as they made their way along the bank before climbing up into the woods further behind.

Once it got its feet onto more even ground, the little calf seemed a lot more confident and bounded off amongst the trees, followed by his mother. As I moved my binoculars along, following this family adventure, a patch of out-of-focus, bright blue appeared in my field of view. I readjusted my focus wheel and the crisp image of a kingfisher on a rock appeared before me.

The rock on which the bird sat was part of a natural, weir-like structure: a line of rocks extending part-way across the river, separating a deeper, slow-flowing section of water from a shallower, more rapidly moving stretch. This feature had trapped several logs and tree trunks uprooted during winter storms, creating a logjam extending from the boulders and into the bank. It had raised the level of water to make a waterfall as the river dropped over the rocks to the level below.

The rich and vibrant colours of the kingfisher were a striking contrast to the brown and black tones of the water, rocks and sodden timber that made up the backdrop for this riverine jewel. It sat there, a tiny, hunchbacked shape, and bobbed its head and body up and down. The sunlight flickered over its deep, blue forehead and crown, which were bedecked with sparkling, diamond-white spots.

Its wings displayed dark-navy spots on a blue background. The tail, in this light, defied my ability to attribute a word to convey the colour – was it turquoise, aquamarine, azure, ultramarine? Whichever it was, it glowed with such intensity that it looked to be illuminated from within, as though the spirit of the bird resided in the tail instead of the heart.

By comparison, the orange underparts were more uniform than the miscellaneous sparking tints of the upper parts. The contours of the feathers created dimples in the bird's plumage which, combined with the colour, reminded me of the skin on a clementine. From beneath the bird's breast feathers protruded two sealing-wax-red feet.

Even allowing for the bird's small stature, those feet still looked ridiculously disproportionate in size. The long, pointed, spear-like bill glistened like a dark ebony shaft. Its uniform black colour indicated that this was a male.

As I watched him, the mother deer and her shaky-legged calf having long since melted into the woodland undergrowth, he called several times: *cheeee ... cheeee ... cheeee*. Taking off, he flew downstream, his small, rounded wings whirring like a beetle's. Kingfishers are so fast-flying that a small flash of colour darting over the river surface is usually all that I would see; there was normally no chance to raise the binoculars. He disappeared around a bend in the river, behind a large, overhanging willow tree, and was gone.

I began to wonder whether my pursuit of this bird was cursed. It was hard to forget that on both occasions when my liberty had been curtailed – through no fault of my own – I had been birdwatching. Although it was a foolish and irrational thought, it made me apprehensive to return to the nest site. Even more distressing was the fact that I was beginning to gain less and less satisfaction from observing them. I spent more time watching the phone than the nest, and my gaze was being directed ever more inwards: deeper and downwards.

But the opportunity the kingfishers were providing me with was one that might not be repeated for some time. Whereas the woodpeckers had nested in the Spanish chestnut tree for many consecutive years, the kingfishers might not ever nest here again. I refocused on the task, and over the coming weeks made several more visits.

Initially my heart was not in it, but, as in the past when circumstances felt insurmountable, I sought the 'silence' of nature to help me rebalance: and the sound of the river, as it rippled, laughed and trickled through the dappled, viridian light, blanketed out the sounds in my head. Returning to the kingfishers gave me a purpose. It grounded me, providing continuity, routine and a sameness – and, although I suspect it would have driven others almost to insanity with frustration, it was what I needed.

The activity at the nest increased considerably following the hatching of the chicks. I was no longer subjected to forty- or fifty-minute waits between birds' appearances as had been the case during incubation. Although the featherless chicks needed brooding during the first few days, the temperature inside the nesting tunnel was sufficient to prevent them from getting chilled during their parents' absences. Because of this, both parents were actively hunting within a day or two of the chicks' arrival.

It was impossible for me to estimate the number of chicks that lay concealed in the bankside opposite me. I could, of course, undertake a similar procedure to that which my friend and I had carried out at the woodpeckers' nest, but doing so from the water carried a lot more risk than doing so on a secured ladder. More importantly, the fragile nature of the clay tunnel, compared to the robustness of the woodpeckers' wooden nesting cavity, may not have survived such an intrusive procedure.

So, although I had a licence from the NPWS for this type of work, I decided there was nothing to be gained and much to lose. Until this year, I had not known how many eggs were in a woodpeckers' nest, but that had not prevented years of enjoyment studying them.

I knew from studies carried out in England that most kingfishers usually had between four and seven young, and sometimes as many as ten. But these were the same sources that referred to two and three successive broods per season. The Wicklow Mountains were different, and I felt it more likely that four or five chicks were in the riverbank – and while a second brood was possible, I would be satisfied if they successfully fledged this one.

Both parents were extremely active in their hunting pursuits, and I regularly encountered one or other of them as I made my way to my chosen vantage point. It was a delightful sight, watching them speeding along the river, the sunlight glinting off the silvery fish held tightly in their bills. After many weeks of lean and meagre entries in my field diary, I was finally being kept busy:

### 4th June

0730   Arrived at watchpoint #1, bird on perch outside nest, flew off upstream at my arrival.

0734   Male arrived from upstream carrying single fish. Fish very small, flew straight to nest entrance and left a minute later flying upstream.

0741   Male arrived and perched outside nest for 20 seconds, before flying off downstream.

0746   Female arrived from downstream carrying a fish. Landed on branch before flying into nest. Re-emerged carrying a faecal sack and flew downstream ...

**5th June**

2130    A pair of goosanders has just landed on the river right in front of me! Amazing sight, preening only metres in front of me, completely at ease and unaware of me ... the echoing tones of a song thrush in the tree above ... hardly any other sound other than the soothing murmuring of water.

2139    Female kingfisher landed on willow tree downstream, preening in last of sun's rays ... everything is at ease this evening ...

The parents were actively feeding their young from at least 5 am, and possibly much earlier, and continued to do so until after 10 pm. By my calculations, based on the frequency of observations made during my visits, I estimated that as many as one hundred fish were being caught each day to feed the hungry chicks. This excludes what the adults caught for themselves.

During the first week, the fish that the adults presented to their hatchlings were small. Most likely these were a mixture of fish fry and three-spined sticklebacks, the latter occurring in slow-flowing parts of the river. However, within a few days, the size of the fish caught by the adults had grown considerably.

Sometimes the adults, carrying their prey, landed on a branch near the nest hole. Even then – and even with a telescope – it was impossible to identify the species of fish being hunted. These larger fish were probably varying-sized specimens of brown trout, as Wicklow's mountain rivers do not have a large selection of fish species and trout are by far the most common.

THE DAYS MERGED into weeks, and still the parents kept up the same routine. Usually alternatively, but not always, one of the parents arrived every ten or fifteen minutes and disappeared into the riverbank. The midsummer plant growth was now at its peak, and the entrance hole to the subterranean nest was all but obscured. With my binoculars I could just about make out the smallest crescent of a circular hole in the riverbank ... but only just.

A screen of ferns, brambles, grasses and other bankside vegetation hung down like a green curtain and screened the kingfishers' nest from all but the sharpest of eyes. White, frothy plumes of meadowsweet grew all along the riverbank. Their intoxicating, musky scent hung heavily in the air: a scent of high summer and of riverbanks.

The fact that the nest hole was almost completely obscured by vegetation may have been a good thing for the young birds' safety, but for me it was a disappointment. In the final few days before leaving the nest, young kingfishers have often been observed coming to the entrance hole to be fed by the parents. In this they are no different to young great spotted woodpeckers.

Having seen many woodpecker family portraits over the years, depicting parents with their young at the nest, it was natural to hope for the same with the kingfishers. When searching for the nest site several months earlier, I had, in my usual optimistic manner, expected it to be in an exposed riverbank, presenting no difficulties for a well-hidden observer.

But the almost completely hidden entrance to the nest meant that there was very little chance of seeing the young birds before they left it. Nest studies in England suggest that the young birds leave the nest after about twenty-five days, a similar length of time to the great spotted woodpecker chicks. In a similar manner, the day of departure – D-Day – can be calculated by the manner in which the young kingfishers sit at the entrance to the burrow. I would not be granted that privilege this season.

By the end of the second week, there were sounds coming out of the nest burrow, audible from where I sat on the far riverbank. When the parents arrived with the fish, which were now quite large, and disappeared into the nest, a chattering noise could be heard. It was quite faint, and I was grateful that, as with my sense of smell, I had good hearing. I have often been surprised when other people are unable to hear the bird calls and sounds of other living creatures that I can.

Several years ago, I was walking with a friend in the late evening down the garden, when I disappeared into the undergrowth saying, 'I can hear a hedgehog in here somewhere.' To their utter amazement, I showed them the hedgehog sitting under a dense patch of brambles. My friend's face was one of disbelief as I explained that, although we had been talking, I had recognized the faint snuffling sounds it made as it foraged for food.

Possibly the noises these young kingfishers made were inaudible to other people, but they told me that the hungry brood was growing, and that D-Day was now not far away. Strangely, unlike the woodpecker chicks, the sounds did not change much over the following week, either in intensity or pitch. They gave no indication of when the chicks might leave the nest.

The adults kept up their consistent routine of bringing food every ten minutes or so. Sometimes they would fly straight past me, hovering momentarily like bejewelled hummingbirds, before disappearing into the undergrowth. Other times, they would fly past and land on one of several conveniently located perches. There they would survey the river before disappearing into the nest.

IT WAS NOW approaching the end of what I believed to be the third week of the kingfisher chicks' subterranean lives. I did not know the exact date of their hatching, and the total number of days they would spend in the nest was an additional variable. Attempting to calculate the day they would leave was therefore a futile affair. The best I could do was simply to watch the nest as often as possible and for as long a period as I could manage within any given day.

The sun was not due to set for another hour or so as I made my way along the bank that evening. I had already spent several hours, earlier in the day, sharing the river with my feathered family of friends. However, I wanted to close the day with a few more sightings; I also just wanted to go for a walk along the river, for no other purpose than to hear it.

Skimming low over the water, its wings almost shearing the water's surface like a blade, a kingfisher sped past me. A flash of orange, an explosion of blue, and it was gone. As I got closer to the nest, I heard a kingfisher calling, but I was unable to locate it. Lying down on the grass and scanning the opposite bank with my binoculars, I glimpsed a kingfisher flying away and disappearing upriver.

I was just about to stand up and move further along the bank to my usual watching spot when I saw movement in a small patch of waterside rushes. Focusing my binoculars, I realized there was another kingfisher. But this one, I felt, was behaving distinctly oddly. It was sitting neither still nor quietly, but instead was scrambling around amongst the rush stems.

Using its tiny feet, it was grasping the weak and unsupportive stems, furiously flapping its wings to keep itself upright. Realizing that the stems could never support its weight, the bird dropped down into the densest part of the tussock. It sat there looking around, appearing slightly confused, before once again trying to scale the vegetation around it. Eventually, through a combination of determination and good fortune, it reached the top.

Launching itself from this precarious and insecure platform, the bird flew rather uncertainly across the river and upstream, before being lost to view ...

The young kingfishers had left the nest.

# ON THE BANKS
# OF THE RIVERS

GENTLY, EVER SO gently, the petals on the wild dog roses in the hedgerows were falling. Unnoticed, and without any last hurrah, they dropped off, one at a time. For the past few weeks, the hedgerows, with their multitude of shades and tints of green, had been delicately covered with splashes of pink and white. The large, five-petalled flowers had an appealingly simple structure, far removed from the complexity of the modern-day cultivars they gave rise to. They filled the evening air with a faint, sweet smell during the warm midsummer evenings, a subtle scent that made it all the more appreciated by those who sought it out.

But the rose is one of our final hedgerow flowers to bloom, and as the petals begin to fall they mark the change of the seasons more definitively than any human calendar. Midsummer had quietly passed by, and we were now beginning the gentle walk into autumn; but no, not yet a walk – an amble, perhaps. The passing of the rose is only rendered bearable by the blossoming of that ultimate of the hedgerow bloomers, the honeysuckle. And what a climax it brings to late-summer evenings.

The still evening air on the riverside banks hung heavy with the sweet, honey-like scent of the woodbine, as the honeysuckle is sometimes known as. For a brief week or so, these two plant species, the crowning glory of the summer hedgerow, play together in the long evenings. Entwined amongst each other and any other vegetation they can cling to, they duck, dive and scramble through the luscious summer growth. But by the end of June their time is through, and – one by one, day by day – the rose quietly sheds its petals and carpets the ground below. And then, a change comes over the hedgerow: it dulls in tone, deepens in colour and sometimes, like myself, even darkens ... as though the light had gone out.

But although the seasons marched relentlessly onwards, sometimes instilling a feeling of panic within me, there was little time to brood or be trapped by the intricate web in which my quest for the kingfisher had somehow become entangled. Now that the young kingfishers had left the nest, I could not afford the luxury of wallowing in despair. The days were long, but time was short – the youngsters were exploring their new, brightly coloured world, and I was eager to explore it with them.

The breeding season of the kingfisher was finally drawing to a close, yet so much remained unanswered. I was still on a voyage of discovery and new lands surely awaited me over the horizon, albeit at that moment out of reach.

This jewel of the river, this speeding, blue bullet – this *spirit* – still captivated me. I remained enthralled. But while closure on the kingfishers and woodpeckers unfortunately eluded me, a resolution to more determinative matters approached, steadfastly and unceasingly. I was in some ways glad that the kingfishers occupied less of my time now, as my mind was finding it ever more difficult to concentrate, let alone enjoy, the natural world around me.

The birds, animals, flowers and other creatures that had for so many years shared my waking moments had begun to lose their lustre several months earlier, with the events that had unexpectedly intruded into my quest like an unwelcome and unshakeable companion. But now, with the approaching finality, they had become enshrouded in what I can only describe as the blackness – *nada*, nothingness – which was driving away not only the kingfisher but everything that this bird represented to me.

In many ways, the birds of the river were as much part of that court hearing as I was. They had been with me when I was arrested, and they were with me, at least in my mind, when I entered the courtroom that morning. The surrealness they brought was almost welcome. The feeling of living in an alternative reality had continued as I spent much of the time with the accompanying gardaí happily discussing my dog, which had remained faithfully by my side in the station that morning.

One of them, sitting beside me, said, 'I hate court.'

'So do I,' I replied.

In the same manner as I scrutinized the feathers on a young woodpecker to identify individuals, we scrutinized the events in micro-detail. As a naturalist, I was a student of detail, but the day's events had bordered on the ridiculous. My mind wandered, and I began to lose focus, followed by interest.

I thought of Excalibur and the knight Parzival's quest for the Holy Grail. I thought of the myth of the halcyon and the kingfisher incubating its eggs in the calmness between the storms that had washed both it and its eggs into oblivion. Drowned by chaos. And I thought of Hecate the witch and her two sisters, who had brought chaos and maelstrom into my world, until my reverie was broken by the word 'kingfisher' followed by 'woodpeckers and other birds'.

In a case of ridiculousness and absurdity, and probably to many people's silent bemusement that morning, the kingfisher and woodpecker had entered the case and momentarily taken centre stage.

And then, in mid-sentence, their lustre returned in a blaze of colour, like a rising sun on a midsummer's day, and the *nada* that had haunted me throughout the preceding months was swept away with a statement, cutting everybody short:

'Look, I'm dismissing this, there's no evidence here at all.'

That same evening, I watched the kingfisher, perched on a willow branch overhanging the river. As the sun set, dipping below the horizon, the bird glowed with an inner light, extending a stabilizing force into the world around me.

IT WAS EARLY in the morning as I pushed my way through the forest of bracken. The sun had climbed over the distant woodland horizon several hours prior, and the air was warm, vibrating to the endless hum of countless flying insects. It flooded my mind, mesmerizing me if I listened too closely. It was the sound of late June, as ubiquitous as the sound an overhead power cable sometimes makes. Insects are one of the powerhouses of the natural world, and even my kingfisher family relied on them, since the fish upon which they were reared had fed on both flying insects and their larvae.

The bracken was now so tall that some fronds towered to head height, and in places higher still. Whereas in the springtime I could walk along the very edge of this riverbank, all the while scanning ahead of me for birds, now I was enclosed in a dense forest that completely shielded the river from my gaze. I had to keep forcing my way out onto the bank, then scan left and right to check for birds, before retreating into a hidden world filled with imagination, innocence and mystery.

This was not an ideal way to watch kingfishers, as it meant I could very easily emerge alongside a bird without sufficient time to conceal myself before being spotted. This had already happened with a goosander. The unfortunate bird, a female, had been resting close to the shore when I had unexpectedly appeared on the bank, only a few metres away. I have wondered how broad a vocabulary these birds possess, since, unlike many other species of duck, they rarely call.

Utterly startled, she tried to swim, run and fly at the same time, all the while making a sound best described as someone retching loudly, rather than anything resembling a quack. Panic-stricken, her bright, orange legs flailed against the water and her wings beat frantically as she twisted her neck around to look at the apparition that had materialized beside her. Having ploughed a froth-filled furrow across the river, she eventually managed to get herself airborne. And, with several more guttural sounds that no bird book has ever attempted to describe, she wheeled over the oak trees and disappeared.

Having frightened her, I was all too conscious that I could easily do the same to the kingfishers. When they were still in the nest, I was able to plan my route and take up a suitable vantage point. But now that they had left the nest, they quickly moved along the banks for several hundred metres either side of their burrow. I started taking more care as I approached the stretch of river they frequented. Still hidden, I would crouch down and crawl on my belly through the final, bamboo-like forest of stems, emerging onto the bank like a lizard creeps from surrounding vegetation onto a stone to begin sunning itself.

The first few times I performed my commando-style manoeuvres proved unproductive, apart from the memorable occasion when a grey wagtail flitted up into the air and darted around catching flies like a tiny water sprite. With its tail fanned, its cheerful calls and bright colours, it was as close to watching a fairy as one could get.

Shortly thereafter, when I parted the next curtain of undergrowth, I had to bite my lip to stifle my breath: there, barely two metres in front of me, sat not one, but two kingfishers.

Fortunately, they had not yet seen or heard me. This part of the river was marked by a dead tree, which had been washed down by winter storms and was now firmly wedged against the bank, a tortured and tangled mass of twisted, broken roots and branches. The birds sat not on the outer boughs of the tree, facing the water, but rather on the side closest to me, hidden from any prying eyes on the water or from the far bank, but completely in my view.

I realized that these were two of the young birds. The blue on their crowns and wings was not as vivid as it was on the adults and also lacked its vibrancy. They sat, like two lonely children, huddled against each other, one wing touching that of the other. Completely without invitation, an image of two lost children being watched by the wolf formed in my mind.

I dared not move, despite the uncomfortable crouching position I was in, in case it alerted them to my presence. Completely unaware of me, they bobbed their heads in that delightful manner of kingfishers. Sometimes in unison, other times in alteration; it was like a comical puppet show that just needed a musical score to set it off to perfection. Although I had on previous occasions managed to see kingfishers as closely as these two, never had I enjoyed such prolonged views. Time seemed to stand still as I drank in their beauty.

Despite lacking the brilliance of their parents, which they would presently attain, their plumage was nevertheless stunning. Because they were sitting facing away from me, the most iridescent part of the plumage – their backs – lay directly in front of my eyes. The turquoise blaze extended from the back of the crown, from which it was separated by a thin, off-white collar: though pure white on adults, and clearly demarcated, on youngsters the collars are more of a dirty cream, with diffuse borders.

The shimmering colour of their backs extended down and onto their tails, where it merged with the darker blue that formed the tips of their short, stumpy tails. Their wings were far duller than those of the adults, and of a purer blue compared to the parents' sparkling, blue-green plumage, which was bedecked with glittering sequins that their offspring lacked.

Suddenly, the two juvenile kingfishers exploded into activity, sitting upright, stretching out their necks and fluttering their wings with great excitement. Their eager calls filled the air with anticipation: *peeeeee-peeeeee-peeeeee* ... The adult bird, the cause of this celebration, was flying towards us, low over the water. It was travelling along the far bank, disappearing in and out of the dappled shadows cast by the overhanging willows. A flash of colour, then nothing, then another flash as it darted across the glistening puddles of sunlight. Truly it was a spirit, demonstrating its powers of disappearance and reappearance.

As it crossed the river towards us, the light glinted off the silver fish grasped firmly in its beak. Landing on a branch near its two fledglings, it hesitated, disregarding their pleas. Unlike them, it was not facing away from me, but instead was looking straight at me – and it did not seem to be impressed by what it saw. My legs were aching beyond belief at this point: I knew that I could not last much longer and that I would shortly experience a horrendous case of pins and needles. Knowing this, and the fact that I had been spotted by the parent, I uncurled my back.

In that instant the adult, which I now recognized as the female, took off, uttering a shrill whistle. Without hesitation her babies followed, and my indulgence was abruptly ended. I was not concerned that they had flown, for their sharp-eyed mother would never have fed them openly with me standing close by. Most likely, she had taken them to a safer hiding place where they could be fed undisturbed. In the meantime, I finally succumbed to the pain of my returning circulation.

JULY IS A strange time of year for me – and this year even more so, as I struggled within myself. Although it was high summer, and the rivers, woods, hedgerows and fields were abundant with life, the urgency and drive that I had felt in the spring had been replaced by a feeling that things were 'all over bar the shouting'. There was plenty of activity in the surrounding countryside, but I had failed to achieve many of the ambitions I had set out to achieve.

Fox cubs played in the nearby hay fields, chasing each other with high-pitched meows and yelps – but I had failed to locate their den ...

Great spotted woodpeckers were bringing their recently fledged youngsters to nearby bird feeders from new woodland territories, where I had searched but failed to locate their nests ...

Pine martens were feeding each night with their kits in front of my remote cameras, but I still had no idea where they lived ...

I had spent many of the dark winter evenings looking forward to what is always the busiest time of year, and the result was always the same. You can't be everywhere at once. If you spend weeks trailing kingfishers along endless riverbanks, then you can't devote hours to walking fields and hedgerows seeking out fox dens. If you are out of bed at 4 am to learn how kingfishers or woodpeckers behave at dawn, then you can't track pine martens through moonlit woods at midnight.

And so, as the petals of the wild rose began to shed, carpeting the grass through which I walked, I had to accept that many things would have to hold over until the following year, as they always will. But while July might mark the end of one road, it also opens others.

Now that the breeding season was ending and the kingfishers were starting to disperse away from their natal rivers, I was no longer restricted, as I had been, to the same few kilometres of river. I was free to explore and look for them in the wider landscape. New landscapes beckoned, new realms ... new worlds. Best of all, now that I was no longer restricted to hours in one spot, I could spend the rest of my explorations accompanied by my spotted companion.

The following morning saw us exploring a section of the same river further beyond the breeding territory. I was curious as to whether there were any suitable banks for future years' breeding. We explored for several hours during one of the hottest days of the year. Within a short space of time I became drenched in sweat. I don't cope well in heat, and this was way above my tolerance level.

Dippers and grey wagtails were the only birds of note, and the banks became so thick with vegetation that it was nearly impossible to ascertain any suitability for breeding kingfishers. As I came around a bend, the river's character changed: the surface water slowed and deepened, forming a dark pool filled with twinkling, copper-coloured water. Overhead, the oak trees formed a large natural cupola of branches and leaves, which filtered the intense heat into beams that created hexagonal patterns of light and shade across the water.

Demoiselle damselflies, an elegant member of the dragonfly family, fluttered weakly over the water. These most beautiful of insects are only found over clean, slow-flowing water. With their rich, bottle-green bodies and blue-green wings, they are both instantly recognizable and beautiful to behold. Like woodland fairies in a fantasy world, they danced and fluttered in the dappled sunshine.

To say that the water looked inviting was an understatement, and within moments both myself and my dog were leaving V-shaped wakes in the water as we raced against each other to the opposite bank. The water was surprisingly deep for a mountain river that was so often shallow over considerable distances. In places it was well above head height, but that posed no problem to either of us.

Looking at the kingfishers' realm from this perspective was quite enlightening. My eyes were roughly the same height above the water as a flying kingfisher, and how different the river now looked. I could see further and navigate my course far more easily than I could from the narrow and restricted bankside viewpoints. Vegetation, which looked impenetrably dense from above, resolved itself into a maze of perches and prominences when seen from below. It was but a glimpse into the waterside world the kingfisher inhabited, but it changed my perception, and my appreciation.

Given the intensity of the heat that day, it was a sheer indulgence to simply drift in the cool water. Paddling slowly alongside me, completely at ease in this environment, as most Dalmatians are, she snuffled and snorted her nose through the water. She tried to grab the various bubbles and pieces of foam that floated by. Months of anguish, anxiety, fear – and more – seemed to drift away on the current, aided by her laughing mouth and lolling tongue.

After several more half-hearted races after sticks, and a few tumbles for good measure to finish with, we left the seclusion the pool offered and returned to the riverbank. But the day's heat continued to grow, and eventually I had to admit defeat. Riverbank exploration of this intensity and calibre had finished, for this season at least.

THE LAKE EXTENDED ahead of me without even a ripple to disturb the perfect reflection of the surrounding hills. Carved out by a glacier tens of thousands of years ago, it was framed by high, scree-covered cliffs that formed a chaotic-looking grey waterfall. Scattered up high, amongst this challenging landscape, were patches of stunted oaks and mountain ash trees. Lower down, where the cliffs met the waters and were less steep, isolated Scots pines dotted the shoreline, their reddish bark catching the morning rays.

All of this was mirrored to perfection and in reverse by the perfectly still waters stretching from side to side. In the early-morning light, as I stared towards the distant shore opposite me, I was unable to see the division in the world in front of me – between actuality and reflection, or maybe between reality and imagination? As I investigated the distance, the two worlds merged; the line between them blurred and the boundaries fell away. It became impossible to identify direction and perspective. Nature reflects the real world against ours – in the natural world, we can lose ourselves.

Glaciated lakes are not favoured haunts of kingfishers. They rarely provide any suitable bank for them in which to excavate their nesting burrows, and the steep cliff faces offer little in the way of fishing perches. Furthermore, they are usually quite deep, even at the edges, and their cold depths harbour less suitable prey for a kingfisher than that species' more usual river haunts. But this lake, like many glacial lakes within the area, was fed by a stream and gave rise to another. In time, it would join with the Avonmore river, on which my kingfisher family lived, which itself had been birthed from another glacial lake many kilometres distant.

This whole region was covered by a vast interlinked fluvial system of waterways – rivers, streams, tributaries, branches, brooks, streamlets, rivulets, burns and many more equally varied forms of flowing water. All of these were the habitat of the birds I had spent the preceding months studying – the dippers, the grey wagtails, the goosanders and, of course, the kingfishers. They used this vast system not just for feeding and nesting, but to travel and disperse. And it was because of their habit of dispersing via this undulating, serpentine highway that, at this time of year, I frequently encountered kingfishers far from their home.

I made my way along the western shore of the lake, cutting through stands of Scots pine, until I reached the far end of the lake. A fast-flowing stream had travelled down for some distance from the heather- and scree-covered mountainside above me. Untamed in its behaviour and sparkling in the sunshine, it filled the air with its bright and breezy banter, before mellowing and merging into the lake beside me with a distinguished silence. I was walking along the last one hundred metres of its journey, in which it was laid out like a long, broad, fat serpent, when a clear-sounding whistle cut through the river's unrestrained noise.

I scanned along the river in front of me and there, on a cascade of rocks, was a kingfisher. The boulder on which it sat was the size of a car, dwarfing the squat, little shape on top of it. Its neck was hunched into its body, its short tail indeterminable since it was pressed flat against the rock. Every ten seconds or so it bobbed its head up and down in the typical kingfisher manner, but otherwise remained motionless. Because it sat rather than perched, its sealing-wax-red feet, which were normally visible, were obscured by the orange feathers of its underparts.

It was without doubt one of the most unusual habitats I had ever seen a kingfisher frequent. Yes, it was near water, but it seemed impossible that a kingfisher could actually feed by diving in amongst these vehicle-sized rocks embedded in the shallow, tumbling waters. But it had little interest in feeding at this moment in time and simply sat, happily bobbing up and down like a multicoloured Jack-in-the-box.

Then it gave its distinctive call, which rebounded off the rocks and, like a ricochet, travelled up, down and across the valley. Cutting through the unceasing song of the mountain gorge, it was clearly audible to those who knew how to listen, yet silent to all others.

I sat and watched for a while, but the scene never changed. Then, very slowly, moving from boulder to boulder – and with a surefootedness far removed from any mountain goat – I reduced the distance between us by about two-thirds. Now, from a closer perspective, I could see the slightly muted colouring on the crown and the less-than-gleaming wing feathers. This was a young bird, not one that had left the nest a few days prior, but probably several weeks earlier.

To reach this moorland burn, this bird must have flown from its natal river upstream along increasingly narrowing watercourses, crossing glacial lakes and ultimately making its way to these scree-covered slopes with their dancing and tumbling cascade. At a guess, I figured that there was no suitable breeding habitat for several kilometres. This youngster had simply travelled in the wrong direction and was now moving into ever more unsuitable terrain.

It continued to call periodically, but no answer ever returned – its parents and siblings were nowhere nearby. I adjusted my position to relieve my cramping legs, and when I looked back it was gone. Which direction it had flown was a mystery: one that I would never solve. Perhaps it had realized that it was effectively on a road to nowhere and had turned back, flying downstream. Leaving the upland watercourses behind, hopefully it would reunite itself with the suitable riparian habitat of its birth.

Alternatively, perhaps responding to some urge buried deep within its genes, it had continued to be driven, compelled or perhaps even called further and further away from its birthland. Following an ever-diminishing series of waterways into increasingly more barren landscapes, it would eventually reach the river's source … and the end.

The river below me was far removed from the stream I had visited previously in that same glaciated valley. This water was flowing between two vertical walls of rock. Although inspiring and impressive as any natural feature, this gorge had been carved not by the forces of nature but by the hand of man. It was shaded from the sun, both by the trees high above and the sides of the gorge itself.

The walls that hemmed in the water were dark and glistened in the perpetual dampness. Several different species of fern clung tenaciously to whatever foothold they had managed to find there: Hart's-tongue lived alongside hard- and soft-shield ferns, together with the bearers of other ostentatious-sounding names.

Thick strands of ivy reached down into the open space from the woodland above and hung, like rainforest lianas or mountaineers' climbing ropes, above the water's surface. Broken and torn boughs from the trees above lay scattered along the river's edge, wedged between the stones in the riverbed and the solid granite buttresses. An occasional mountain ash sapling sprouted from where the river had deposited a bed of silt against the wall. There, in the smallest excuse for a beach, the saplings had taken root and extended their roots deeper into the riverbed, and from thence into the bedrock.

There was a strange, almost prehistoric feel to this site. It looked more suited to the landscapes in Jules Verne's *Journey to the Centre of the Earth* than County Wicklow. With no clay banks in which to excavate burrows, this was not a suitable breeding habitat for kingfishers. Dippers, however, found this river very much to their liking, and a pair had bred here for many years, building their nest deep within a culvert that carried this river under a nearby road.

This deep, narrow, granite-framed auditorium provided an astounding acoustic experience, unrivalled by any other river I knew. Like all Irish dippers, the birds on this river sang throughout the year – even now, in July. Territories are maintained all year round by the male, although the female often wanders further afield during the non-breeding months.

The song that rose from that cleft in the earth was rich, pure and clear, but, most of all, it was *loud*. The dipper was standing on a rock in the middle of the river, its bill tilted so far upwards that it appeared to be leaning backwards to keep its balance. Its song reverberated back and forth off the ravine-like structure, gaining strength, creating echoes, echoes of echoes. When it finally erupted into the woodland above, it was almost impossible to identify direction or duration – just like when listening to classical music, it can be hard to identify the separate parts of an orchestra.

The song of the dipper is naturally loud and clear, so that it can be heard above the sound of the rushing, churning water that is its home. It carries so well on the wind that I have often heard it while in a car, driving over a bridge. However, the song that emerged from below me today was of a calibre far beyond what would be considered usual. Every note, every nuance and variation, was equally audible. The natural acoustics of this setting had amplified the low notes and mellowed the high notes, creating a unique symphony of staggering beauty ... for which I was the sole audience member.

As I watched the bird far below me with my binoculars, standing on its small, glistening-wet and moss-encrusted song post, I could see that it was watching me as I gazed upon its tuxedoed plumage. It cocked its head sideways so that one of its beady eyes was directed straight at where I stood. How it knew I was there fascinated me, since I would have failed to spot it were it not for the soaring crescendo of sound that it was producing. As it continued to sing and to look up at me, I could see it blinking, its white eyelids clearly visible in the gloomy light of the cutting.

I have long been fascinated by birds' eyes. We are supposedly a superior species – the dominant and most advanced on earth – yet our senses pale when compared to those found elsewhere in nature. Kestrels, sadly a rapidly declining species in Ireland, are but one example of animals with amazing senses: in this instance, eyesight. Watching a kestrel, the windhover of Gerard Manly Hopkins' famous poem, is an awe-inspiring experience, and one I often enjoyed as a boy while lying on my back on the banks of the river on warm summer days … and still do.

It hangs in the air, perhaps forty or fifty metres above the grassy landscape, like a Maltese cross. No matter what the wind, it maintains a stationary pose, regulated by miniscule adjustments of its wings, tail and head. It constantly tweaks for every variation in the air currents: a small twist of its black-tipped tail, a brief flick of its russet wings or a tiny jerk of its body. All the time, its head is pointed downward, its eyes riveted to the grass below.

The kestrel feeds primarily on rodents, most often wood mice. We know from studies that this small raptor can identify the presence of rodents by the urine trails they leave along the ground. However, how it spots these tiny creatures, scurrying half-hidden amongst the grass, from so high up is as big a mystery now as it was when I was a boy. I challenge anyone, even using artificial enhancements such as binoculars or telescopes, to spot a small and almost completely hidden rodent from fifty metres' distance. What their eyes perceive is astounding: their resolution, magnification and sensitivity to movement – and perhaps even to body heat – puts many of mankind's 'achievements' to shame. So many of our so-called discoveries are nothing more than a sudden, simple understanding of nature's creations. Electricity, optical enhancement, sonar, flight and so many more 'inventions' all existed in nature long before we descended from the trees and first began walking out across the plains of Africa to begin our global domination.

My reverie and reflection on the wonders of the world about me were broken as the dipper ended its performance and flew off upstream, uttering its metallic *zink* call. As my eyes followed its departure, I noticed an unusual disturbance along the water's edge further upriver. Curious, I went to get a closer look, and, as I did so, to my surprise a kingfisher flew out of the broken willow tree overhanging the mysteriously rippling and splashing waters.

It surprised me because this was not a typical riverine habitat for a kingfisher. The banks were predominantly granite, and there was no clay into which to burrow. The river itself was, by kingfisher standards, shallow, as well as being rocky with a stony bed. Any kingfisher trying to live here would not be able to engage in its usual, spectacular deep-dives – not unless it wanted to seriously damage itself by crashing into the riverbed. But there was no denying its existence, whistling as it shot downstream in a blaze of colour. Blue … orange … and then blue again as it banked and twisted until out of view.

I turned my attention back to the mysterious disturbance along the river's edge. Through my binoculars I could see the cause: fish. Not just one or two fish, but hundreds and hundreds of fish, scrambling, squirming, thrashing and wriggling for many metres along the cliff-like riverbank. They were spawning.

Although the river was hemmed in by solid granite walls, it still had a gradient from the centre, so that in parts there was a gravel-like shore where miniature waves lapped against the rocky sides. It was this shallow gravel bed that had attracted the shoals of fish, enticing them back to what was quite likely their birthplace. And, in turn, this bonanza of food had lured the kingfisher away from its more usual haunts and into this half-lit, almost mythical landscape.

How the kingfisher had found this living buffet puzzled me. Fish-spawning was a short-lived affair, lasting at most a couple of days, often considerably less. An unpredictable event, it was thought to be linked to the cycles of the moon and other events which affect many creatures' circadian rhythms. But what of the kingfisher? I could not believe that this was a regular daily haunt of this bird, given that far more suitable and reliable hunting grounds lay not too far away. Did the same events which triggered the spawning cause a stirring in the kingfisher's own blood and cause it to seek out what were otherwise unsuitable feeding grounds? These are questions which will in all likelihood never be satisfactorily answered, either by myself or any other naturalist.

But discovering the rich food source was only the first part of the puzzle concerning the kingfisher. How did it actually *catch* the fish? I studied them intently, but due to the distance, and also the fact that they were as densely packed together as sardines in a tin, it was hard to discern much detail. They were quite small, about three-quarters the length of my little finger, and there were flashes of red, black and gold as they fought amongst the shallows, but their exact identity eluded me. So shallow was the water that many of them were half out of the water, with their backs and dorsal fins well above the surface; others were half-beached, wriggling desperately to return to their watery world.

Watching them doing this made me realize that the kingfisher I had just seen most likely had no need actually to dive into the water to catch its prey: it could have easily landed at the water's edge and grabbed a fish as it lay half-trapped, absorbed in its struggle to reproduce. In fact, it could easily have caught enough fish in a couple of minutes to satisfy its hunger for much of the day. I have never heard reports of kingfishers fishing from the shore like this, simply picking off fish as they lay exhausted, but I could think of no other way for it to catch them; unless, of course, it was mere coincidence that it was there with the fish, but I thought not.

The woodlands that surrounded this river played host to many species of bird: some, like the robin, familiar to the general public;

others, such as the treecreeper, considerably less so. Birds like the kingfisher attract admiration for their colours and their impressive hunting ability. But other birds are equally impressive, yet go almost unnoticed by many people, save for the occasional and briefest of encounters. And none more so than our truly nocturnal species, the owl. Like the kingfisher, where a brief glimpse of colour can set the pulse racing, so an encounter with a silent-winged, ghostly apparition can sear itself onto the mind's eye and lure one away from the light and into the shadows.

THE JULY FULL moon was slowly rising over the oak trees on the hillside opposite where I lay in the long summer grass. It hung, precariously balanced on the topmost branches, like a giant tangerine, its colour gradually changing from almost orange to rich cream and eventually to white as it climbed steadily towards its zenith. The sun had set almost an hour beforehand, and the air was still warm from the day's heat. It hung heavy, infused with the scent of the meadow grass beneath me, the perfume of honeysuckle from the hedge behind me and that indefinable aroma of cooling air mixing with the crepuscular landscape, for me one of the most intoxicating of all scents.

I had spent most of the day watching the young kingfishers explore the world around them like a group of excited children. Satisfied with my exploits, I had begun to make my way homeward, but my time was my own that day and home felt far away, albeit only figuratively. I was reluctant to leave, for no other reason than I simply did not want the day to end. I was like a child who just didn't want to go to bed. Time was too short and life too precious to waste in sleep: there was an eternity waiting for that. So, leaving the kingfishers to settle safely for the night amongst the riverside vegetation, I continued along the river until I found the open patch of grass where I now lay – listening to the sounds of the river, watching the imperceptible movement of the moon treading softly on the treetops and feeling the scented, cooling air drifting over my face.

After the sun had set, while waiting for the moon to creep over the woodland rim, I stared at a sky that almost defied belief – or if not belief, then description. The western sky was ablaze with yellow. No, not yellow: yellows.

Every tint, shade and gradient were represented across the expansive palette in front of my eyes, and that was just for the yellows. Then came the reds and the oranges. And as for the blues ...

It was overwhelming ... and truly magical.

As the earth continued its rotation the light continued to fade, and the colours deepened as they began their transformation into the monochrome of night-time. Lying there in the half-light, I felt that I had left the earth and travelled to an unknown land ...

And then I heard it.

A loud and long-drawn-out wail, not unlike the sound a rusty gate makes as it swings back and forth. However, this was no gate: it was the sound of a bird I knew well, the cry of a young long-eared owl calling out to its parents as it waited to be fed. And, furthermore, the owlet was not alone. From several other trees came answering calls as its siblings, roused by the fading light, announced to their silent, hidden parents that they too were hungry.

Mostly the calls were coming from high up in a small group of Scots pines, conifers being the preferred habitat for this species. However, unexpectedly, I suddenly heard one calling from behind me, and from close by too. Surprisingly, it sounded near ground level. I slowly rolled over onto my chest and, without raising my head, peered upwards through the long grass surrounding me. In the gloomy light I was able to make out a large western gorse bush, on top of which sat the young owl.

Through my binoculars, even in this rapidly deepening twilight, I could see its dark facial mask and cryptic markings. Looking straight at me with its orange-coloured eyes, it arched its neck and, throwing its head backwards like a wolf howling, let forth a loud, long cry – but there was no response to its demand.

Following a few more solo renditions, the owl took off and glided ever closer on silent wings until it alighted on a broken branch on a small, twisted and gnarled hawthorn in front of me. Once again it arched its head and called – a mournful cry from the soul – but again its pleas went unanswered. Taking off, it flew soundlessly over my head and melted into the velvet darkness that was its world.

The Fisher King and the owl: two creatures living in opposite realms of the same world. One a jewel that reflects the day's light and scatters its warmth across the water, the other cloaked in darkness and shining in the moon's cold glow. Like the human brain, with its two hemispheres working to create a single thought, the world around us has many facets that unite to form our life's experiences ...

We simply need to learn that which we have forgotten.

# AFTERWORD:
# RAINBOW BRIDGE

A LOT OF water had flowed under that bridge since my father and I had watched the river's spirit flying past us ... a lot of water.

The old battlement bridge is still there, with the ruined abbey dominating the horizon, and kingfishers still frequent that verdant, almost mythical world which my father and I shared and explored together. But, in harmony with the flowing of the river, it has become less hidden and more frequented. The world has moved on.

The bridge upon which I was standing also bore testimony to the passing of time on a scale not measured in numbers. It was not a battlement bridge, yet the cut-stone walls that framed the narrow, grass-covered deck reached head height and restricted the view to those old enough not to understand it.

The granite twinkled in the autumn sunshine, the countless shards of mica embedded in the stone's matrix reflecting the light like a dazzling display of miniature fireworks. Small ferns clung to the stonework, creating a miniature canopy. A whole new world existed there, on a different scale and on a different level to ours. On the far side of the bridge, on the banks of the river, stood a small church. A far cry from the grandeur of the abandoned abbey that dominated the skyline in my youth, it was dwarfed by the towering majesty of the surrounding landscape. I scanned along the river's edge, hoping for a glimpse of blue ... but there was none.

'WAIT,' I SAID, 'I think I see a dipper!'

'Daddy, I can't see *anything*!' came the frustrated reply, 'Lift me *up*!' As I lifted my nine-year-old son up to see the bird, time fell away – a feeling of déjà vu, mingled with alternate realities, swam through my head. Bridges ... churches ... rivers ... kingfishers ... father and son ... but then the feeling of being trapped in an inescapable circle was broken by the addition of another voice.

'Dada,' cried my six-year-old daughter, 'I can't see *either*!'

The same but different.

There was not just one dipper, there were three; but the youngsters had all moulted into adult plumage, and it was impossible to say which were the parents and which were the offspring. We watched the dippers together, one family watching the other in an autumn setting as resplendent and superlative as anywhere in the world.

The water level in the river was low, and it sparkled, twinkled and laughed its way amongst the sunlit rocks of the riverbed. The valley rose up steeply on either side of us, and the trees had responded to the steadily shortening daylight with an imposing panorama of colour. Shades of auburn, gold, russet, yellow and orange expanded into tangerine, chocolate, ginger, chestnut and countless other tints and tones for which no description had yet been fashioned. The canvas upon which they had been displayed was a cerulean blue, dotted randomly with white cotton-ball puffs of cloud.

The dippers fed together, but independently, in the shallow water upstream from the bridge. Here they rummaged amongst the gravel riverbed, their heads submerged as they foraged under the stones for insect larvae. Every few seconds they raised their heads for a quick breath and to swallow their prey, before plunging back underwater. The water fell off their heads and ran along the contours of their bodies. Glittering ball-bearings and glassy spheres rolled down the gullies and furrows of their waterproofed feathers before being channelled into the air and shattering below, on impact, into oblivion.

The autumn sunshine turned what, on overcast days, simply looked like a black-and-white bird into a mixture of dark compounds. A cocoa-coloured head blended into sooty-black upper parts, while a thin band of burnt sienna separated the throat, with its colour of freshly fallen snow, from the pitch-black underparts. Every now and then, one of them would utter its metallic *zink* call – a call which had accompanied me along the riverbanks for so many months as I followed the lives of these fascinating birds. In fact, it was a sound that had followed me since I was a boy exploring the riverbanks while lying on my belly. As we watched them from the bridge, my son unexpectedly voiced his feelings, and mine, as he so often did.

'They are seriously awesome birds,' he exclaimed, and I couldn't have agreed more.

His younger sister then contributed, by moving our thoughts onwards and expanding our imagination as only she can.

'Where does this bridge go?' she queried. I was about to jump in with only the black-and-white logical answer that my mind knew, when I paused.

'Where do you think?' I responded.

'Fairyland!' came the reply. 'Or maybe it's the bridge at the end of the rainbow?'

'Rainbow bridge,' I said, thinking of the beautifully written story, almost certainly borrowed from Norse mythology, which had consoled me so many times following the loss of yet another inseparable friend.

In the story, when a much-loved pet dies it goes to a lush green meadow beside a rainbow-coloured bridge where, restored to full health, it wants for nothing and runs and plays all day. Well, it wants for almost nothing, but cannot comprehend what is missing from its seemingly perfect existence. Then, after a long wait, its owner arrives and so they crossed the bridge together, reunited at last and never again to be separated.

A beautiful concept, it had helped me for many years deal with the heartache of inevitable separation, no matter how unlikely the story was. One thing I did know: if by any chance it did come to pass, there would be an awful lot of animals crossing the bridge together with me!

A bridge can link two worlds, even just in our minds, spanning a timeless river. The three of us on the bridge were in the present, and the chaotic world we came from, as we stepped onto the bridge, was in the past. The future – if we were to cross the bridge – lay either in my daughter's fairyland, or more likely a continuation of my search.

A clear-sounding whistle sliced through my senses: Halcyon, the ice bird, the Spirit of the River.

'What's that?' came the inevitable cry from my shoulders.

'Kingfisher!' I shouted above the noise of the water that flowed beneath us. In a flash of colour, the bird flew up from the river over our heads and disappeared behind us, a dazzling, blue dart which vanished downstream, leaving behind nothing but wonder and questions.

It was impossible to have known from that view whether it was one of the adults or one of the youngsters that had graced us with its presence. I suspected, being autumn, that the youngsters had all moved on from their natal territory and were each now venturing far afield in search of their own realm to lay claim to as its spirit. The coming months would undoubtedly claim many of their lives, but such was their existence.

If the winter was a harsh one, then their parents would probably follow them away from this waterway. But, being more experienced, they would most likely survive and sit out the seasonal harshness either in coastal or estuarine haunts. The kingfisher that had flashed past us would probably stay around this area for some months. As challenging as the winter often can be in the Wicklow Mountains, with its inundations of water and sometimes snow, there would be many more weeks of gentle preamble as we wandered through the autumn.

My thoughts on their future were interrupted by far less material questions from beside me.

'The kingfisher is beautiful ... who made it?'

My mind spun. We were like a river delta at the end of our journey, now branching out in a myriad of directions, some of which I did not want to follow. Was this the time for philosophy, for Darwinism, for theology or any other form of explanation?

I looked across the bridge, where the future lay.

It was not fairyland that lay on the far side of the bridge; it was the answer to the question. An answer that could change the effect the kingfisher had just had on their young minds, in the same way it had influenced mine when my father answered the same question on a different bridge, along a different river, in a different world ... or was it?

No, that future was a closure of the realm of innocence, of an open door into a world of light and wonder. They did not need to cross to the other side of the bridge today; there was time enough for that later.

'Does it matter?' I replied, laughing. 'Maybe it was the fairies?'

Instead of crossing the bridge, we stayed on that side of the river and walked downstream along the riverbank in the hope of relocating the kingfisher. The changes brought about by the onset of autumn flowed along with us as we made our way south, away from the bridge. The riverside meadow had lost its summer resplendence and was now a thatch of beige grass. Hedgerow blossoms had been replaced by swollen fruits, and waves of colour swept through the tree canopy, all reflected in the water's ceaseless wanderings.

To our disappointment, there was no sign of the kingfisher, yet I had no doubt it was there somewhere amongst the riverbank foliage, buried deeply amongst the leaves and well hidden from view. It may be a widespread bird – perhaps even common in places – but with few exceptions, it took perseverance on the part of the birdwatcher to get it to reveal its secrets. Often, while watching kingfishers here, I had seen people standing on the bridge looking at the river. They invariably failed to see the bird, and in many cases I suspected they neglected to see the river, let alone its hidden spirit.

Eventually we reached as far as we needed to go and lay there watching the river, the three of us on our bellies and our dog alongside us. A grey wagtail, chasing flies, flittered and fluttered on the opposite shore. It was a blur of activity. Looking through my binoculars, I noted the muted plumage and pale edges to its wing feathers, identifying it as one of this year's young birds.

Explaining the difference, I was interrupted with, 'Why has it got a long tail?' The innocence compared to my unnecessary, in-depth analysis was not lost on me, and I smiled. As always, I thought, we only need remember that which we have forgotten.

The wagtail continued to dance in front of us, flashes of yellow and glimpses of grey amongst an aerobatic performance, a private viewing of the simplest of sights made none the less enjoyable by its everyday status. We lay there, with no sounds around us other than the wistful whisper of the breeze and the rippling tones of the river.

'I like the river,' said my son, 'it quietens my head … it stops the noise.' I knew what he meant. We were so alike in that manner.

'Yes,' I replied, 'it does.'

The kingfisher failed to reappear, and the wagtail soon moved off, but we stayed there. With the year drawing to a close, I thought about the kingfisher. I had started my quest – such a grandiose term for an excuse to roam the riverbanks – with plans and expectations, most of which had failed to materialize. The journey, like the river, had developed many surprising twists and turns, and I had explored much undiscovered country, both around me and within me.


IN THE STORY of King Arthur, the Knights of the Round Table had been questing for the Holy Grail when they encountered the Fisher King: a tangible goal, or so they thought. But although they searched endlessly, they were unsuccessful in their quest, as they failed to recognize the Grail for what it truly represented – as did I in mine. The further they searched, the deeper they travelled into the Waste Land: a dark mental state, a surreal extension of self where man had severed his primal and magical connection to nature and the world around him.

The landscape across which they quested had formerly been fresh, pure and green, as this landscape had been after the ice had retreated and the greenwood extended northwards. But the untainted landscape became a Waste Land as the questors were forced to a realization of the barrenness of their souls, and as they cut themselves off from the source, from nature.

Only after Parzival experienced the inner desolation of no longer being part of nature and underwent his purification through the river did the Grail finally reveal itself to his understanding. As commemorated in John Boorman's magnificent film *Excalibur*: 'Only the pure of heart shall find the Grail.' Stripping himself of his armour, Parzival symbolically sheds the mental darkness that has haunted and tainted him. He allows the river to cleanse his body, soul and mind. He reunites with the primal forces of nature – a physical connection with the world around him that sets him free. In doing so, he leaves the Waste Land and sees the Grail for what it truly represents, and not that for which he had quested.

Perhaps, like Parzival, when I set off to follow the kingfisher, I too had been searching for something I didn't know. I had spent over ten years watching woodpeckers, seven of which were focused on one tree. This was only the first year I had become involved with this family of kingfishers, and it would certainly not be the last. And there were all the other animals whose lives I wanted to share: pine martens, red kites, red squirrels and otters, to name but a few. There was a still a lifetime of wonder for that small boy to explore.

In the light of the setting sun I looked at the river, tasted the air and inhaled the intoxicating scents of the land. More importantly, I looked at my two children beside me, our dog happily squashed between them completing our family. I reflected on the lifeforce – the spirit – of the river and realized that, like Parzival, I too had left the Waste Land and found my Grail.